TIMBER PRESS
POCKET GUIDE TO
Hostas

TIMBER PRESS
POCKET GUIDE TO

Hostas

DIANA GRENFELL
and
MICHAEL SHADRACK

TIMBER PRESS

Published in 2007 by
Timber Press, Inc.
The Haseltine Building
133 S.W. Second Avenue, Suite 450
Portland, Oregon 97204-3527, U.S.A.

www.timberpress.com

For contact information regarding editorial, marketing, sales, and distribution in the United Kingdom, see www.timberpress.co.uk.

Designed by Christi Payne
Printed through Colorcraft Ltd., Hong Kong

Library of Congress Cataloging-in-Publication Data

Grenfell, Diana.
    Timber Press pocket guide to hostas / Diana Grenfell and Michael Shadrack.
        p. cm.
    Includes bibliographical references and index.
    ISBN-13 978-0-88192-847-1
  1.   Hosta. I. Shadrack, Michael. II. Title. III. Title: Pocket guide to hostas.
IV. Title: Hostas.

    SB413.H73G7427 2007
    635.9'3432—dc22
                                        2007002615

A catalog record for this book is also available from the British Library.

Acknowledgments

We should like to thank again all the people and places mentioned in *The Color Encyclopedia of Hostas*, on which this pocket guide is based. Countless individuals gave freely of their knowledge and advice, and allowed unfettered access to their hosta collections. We are especially grateful to the following: Michelle and Tony Avent, Stephen Baker, Gwen Black, Ann and Roger Bowden, Sandra Bond, Leila Bradfield, Chris Brickell, Mary Chastain, Donald Church, Oscar and Peter Cross, Ian Crystal, Margo and Udo Dargatz. Una Dunnett, the late Ed Elslager, Clarence Falstad, Joyce and Marco Fransen, Roger Grounds, Kathy Guest Shadrack, Joe Halinar, Hans Hansen, Kirk Hansen, Jack Hirsch, Jay Hislop, David Howard, Bob Kuk, Gary Lindheimer, Ran Lydell, Bill Meyer, Lu and Dan Nelson, Clarence Owens, Hugo Philips, Warren Pollock, Peg and Ray Prag, Charles Purtymun, Jean and Peter Ruh, Tim Saville, W. George Schmid, Jim Schwarz, Barry Sligh, Nancy and Bob Solberg, Alex Summers, Susan and Alan Tower, The Virginia Tech Entomology Department, Shirley and Van Wade, Kevin Walek, Mary Walters, Jane and Dick Ward, Jerry Webb, James Wilkins, Fred and Audra Wilson, and Mark Zilis.

About This Book

The introduction to this pocket guide provides readers with an overview of hosta botany and basic cultivation. It also describes how hostas are used in the landscape.

The bulk of the book consists of plant descriptions arranged in alphabetical order by scientific name. Each entry is accompanied by a color photo and begins with name of the size category to which the plant belongs—miniature, small, medium, large, or giant—as determined by the American Hosta Society (and explained in the introduction), and the plant's leaf color and type of variegation, where relevant. These general statements make it easy for gardeners to scan through the book and locate a particular type of hosta without having to read every word of the descriptions themselves.

Next come details of clump size and habit, followed by easy-to-understand descriptions of the leaves and flowers.

Cultivation information is presented in the comments following the description and includes light and moisture requirements, growth rate, pest resistance (that is, attractiveness to slugs and snails), and other factors important to the successful growing of each plant. Because most hostas are hardy in USDA zones 3 through 8, hardiness is not mentioned in the individual descriptions unless it deviates from these norms. Many helpful suggestions for using the plants in the landscape are also given in the comments section, augmenting the very helpful lists at the beginning of the book which recommend plants for specific purposes and landscapes.

Finally, each description concludes with the names of plants that are similar to the one just described and/or sports of it. In this way the reader is exposed to 800 choice plants. Names preceded by an asterisk (*) indicate that the plant is fully described elsewhere in this pocket guide.

Rounding out the treatment are hardiness zone maps, a list of further books to read, and another of nursery sources where plants can be obtained.

CONTENTS

Opposite: The garden of Audra and Fred Wilson, Ackworth, Iowa.

PREFACE

Before the 1990s hosta enthusiasts were thirsting for knowledge and were less discerning—or less critical—about the available hostas, rarely discarding any which were considered less than perfect. Now, thanks to the expeditions being undertaken by more and more collectors, breeders, and nursery owners who study hostas in the wild, we know more about the habitats and conditions in which the species live and so are better able to grow both species and varieties more successfully in our gardens.

What is most exciting to the gardener is that hostas are now, and have been for several years, the number one perennial plant in the United States. There are, and always were, excellent reasons for this being so. First and foremost is the sheer sumptuousness of their leaves: they outshine the leaves of every other foliage plant in the garden. There is also the diversity of the size, shape, and color of the leaves, the ease of cultivation, and the quick response to a gardener's care and attention. Hostas have given shade gardening the recognition and cachet it deserves, especially in hot climates, where cool shaded areas are prized over sunny borders. All these qualities have earned hostas their place as the supreme shade plant. Moreover, small and large nurseries as well as tissue-culture laboratories are springing up everywhere, making a huge and ever-increasing range of hostas available to the gardening public.

Opposite: The garden of Philip Little, Waterloo, Ontario, Canada.

INTRODUCTION

Hostas are typically clump-forming perennial plants with broadly or narrowly heart-shaped leaves and clusters of lilylike flowers carried on upright stems just above the foliage. They are easy, adaptable plants that can be grown in most gardens.

Hostas in the Landscape

Hostas are shade-tolerant rather than shade-loving, being native to woodland and forest margins rather than the depths of the forest. Most hostas grow best in open woodland with high, filtered shade and shelter from desiccating winds. Natives of the Far East, their natural companions are oaks and pines, larch and spruce, with an understory of rhododendrons, azaleas, and butcher's broom, as well as Solomon's seal, *Smilacina racemosa*, *Disporum sessile*, ground-covering ivies, and early spring bulbs.

Generally, large groups of hostas with solid-colored leaves of midgreen or gray-blue blend better into a woodland landscape than hostas of brighter hues. Bamboos and ferns, trilliums and asarums also combine well with the less showy hostas in relaxed plantings. More formal public parks and open spaces tend to use hostas as ribbon planting or as an edging in the foreground; *Hosta* 'Chinese Sunrise' is frequently put to this use. Other selections, such as *Hosta* 'Resonance', are used as ground cover, which can also help prevent soil erosion.

Hosta 'Halcyon' with *Viola riviniana*, *Trillium chloropetallum*, and *Lamium galeobdolon* in the Beth Chatto Gardens, Essex, England.

Opposite: Part of the huge hosta collection of Van and Shirley Wade, Belville, Ohio.

A trough planting of small and miniature hostas at Hosta Choice Gardens in Ontario, Canada.

Hostas can be an invaluable ingredient of the mixed border, their leaf outlines being a foil early in the season to strap-shaped hemerocallis and the burnished bronze foliage of peonies; later on, sun-tolerant hostas such as *Hosta* 'Diana Remembered' accentuate the spikiness of yuccas and phormiums. Medium-sized blue-leaved hostas can comfortably share a semi-shaded cottage garden plot placed in front of phloxes like *Phlox* 'Toits de Paris' and purple- or blue-flowered campanulas, the hostas' flowers being an added bonus. Hostas with colored or variegated foliage can be used to draw the eye to or from a particular area or to reinforce a floral color grouping.

The increasing popularity of growing hostas in pots is partly because it is easier to prevent leaf damage by slugs and snails. Generally, it is the larger hostas that look best in pots, but where several pots are grouped together, it is important to vary the size of the hostas as well as their leaf shape and coloring or variegation. Terracotta chimney pots and lengths of underground water pipes help to create versatile and unusual rela-tionships between plant and container. Small and miniature hostas can be successful in containers such as sinks and troughs. They need a sharply draining growing mix which should be placed over a minimum of 3 in. (8 cm) of pea shingle. These hostas should never be divided into very small segments; larger divisions grow away better.

A few hosta species grow naturally in water meadows and other very wet conditions, but these are mostly smaller species and are in scale with the local vegetation. In cultivation the vegetation surrounding ponds or streams is usually too rampant for such hostas, though medium-sized, large, and even giant hostas may be vigorous enough to compete. Few will last for long with their roots directly in the water.

Most hostas have solid leaves with entire margins, so hellebores with their many-fingered leaves, dicentras with their finely divided leaves, and ferns with their lacy fronds afford a contrast, as do sedges and grasses with their linear leaves. Size and texture also matter. Large leaves look

Hostas among other waterside plants at Cambridge Botanic Garden, Cambridge, England.

larger when grown next to small leaves, which makes the small leaves look smaller too.

Hosta Botany

Hostas are frost-hardy perennials with white, fleshy roots. Those with compact root systems produce rounded mounds of foliage, those with running roots irregular spreading patches of foliage. The leaves rise directly from the roots. The flowers are tubular, bell-shaped, flared and funnel-shaped or spider-shaped, usually with six spreading lobes called tepals. They are presented in a raceme on a usually unbranched scape and vary in color from white to deep purple. The reproductive organs consist of six stamens (the male organs), and of a stigma, a style, and an ovary (the female organs). If fertilized, the ovary will swell into an elongated, many-chambered capsule, and seed will mature in about six weeks. Plants start into growth as the ground warms in the spring, withering away at the onset of winter, over-wintering as roots with dormant buds.

Hosta Leaves

The leaves are usually in two distinct parts, the petiole (stalk) and the blade, but in a few hostas they run together (decurrent). The petioles are variously U- or V-shaped and normally the color of the corresponding blade, though often a

The colorful petioles of *Hosta* 'Fire Island' are dotted and streaked with bright red throughout the season.

paler tone; any variegation is carried down into the petiole. Some petioles have distinct red or purple dots.

Most hostas produce juvenile leaves and adult leaves which differ in shape. For the purposes of this book, a mature hosta (one which produces adult leaves) is usually one that has completed its fifth growing season after root division. Many hostas also produce summer leaves that are different from the first leaves of spring. In the directory section of this book, the leaves described are adult leaves unless otherwise stated.

Hosta leaves are classified by size, shape, leaf blade, venation, substance, finish, and color, and these categories are determined by the American Hosta Society, as follows:

Class 1 (Giant) 144 in.^{2} (900 cm^2) and larger
Class 2 (Large) 81–144 in.^{2} (530–900 cm^2)
Class 3 (Medium) 25–81 in.^{2} (160–530 cm^2)
Class 4 (Small) 6–25 in.^{2} (36–160 cm^2)
Class 5 (Miniature) 2–6 in.^{2} (13–36 cm^2)
and smaller

Leaf shape is described in terms of the ratio of length to width: round (1:1), oval (2:1 or 3:2), broadly oval (6:5), elliptical (3:1), and lance-shaped (6:1). In practice the leaves in any one plant may fall between definitions.

The **base** of the leaf, or **lobes** may be heart-shaped, cut straight across, or wedge-shaped, or it may be **decurrent** with the petiole.

The **tip** of the leaf may end abruptly in a sharp point, taper gradually to a sharp point, come straight to a sharp point, or be rounded with a vestigial point.

Leaf margins are normally entire, that is lacking teeth, spines, or lobes though occasionally they may have very slight serrations. They may also be flat, undulate, or evenly and deeply rippled, this being known as "piecrusting."

The **midrib** is lighter in color than the blade, often colorless, and can appear to pierce the blade, particularly in glaucous, self-colored leaves.

The **leaf blade** may be level, undulate, or twisted and can be shallowly or deeply cupped. The surface may also be smooth, dimpled, seer-suckered, puckered, or furrowed. The finish of the blade's upper surface can be matt or shiny, but is usually in-between (satiny).

The **veins** enter the leaf at its base, and curve outward as the leaf widens and inward as the leaf narrows toward the tip. They can appear deeply impressed when seen from above and prominently raised when seen from below.

The area between the veins may be thick or thin, and this is known as **leaf substance** (sometimes incorrectly called texture). The greater the substance, the stiffer and more rigid are the leaves. The leaves are always smooth, that is, without hairs or roughness. Some are glaucous (having a grayish white overlay or waxy coating).

Leaf color of the wild species is normally green, though variegated sports do occasionally occur. All variegation is more or less unstable, but marginal variegation is usually more stable than central variegation.

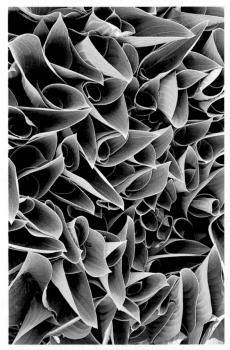

On opening, the leaves of *Hosta* 'Blue Cadet' are an intensely glaucous blue-green.

Flowers

Hosta flowers are borne at the tops of stems (called scapes) which arise directly from the rootstock at the base of the leaf mound. The scapes themselves are usually round and solid, occasionally ridged, and usually simple and rarely branched. They may be upright or leaning, and can be straight or curved. In the plant descriptions, the measurement given for scapes refers to the length, not the height.

The individual flowers are held away from the scape by short stems (pedicels) which may be at a right angle or may allow the flower to droop. The pedicels emerge from flower bracts (modified leaflike structures) which in some species and cultivars are so small that they can scarcely be seen, while in others they are so large they may be mistaken for true leaves. Typically they wither once flowering is over.

Some hostas have a second type of bracts known as foliaceous or leafy bracts, or inflorescent leaves. Leafy bracts can always be distinguished from flower bracts because they occur on the lower part of the scape beneath the flowers. The largest leafy bracts occur toward the base of the scape, and the bracts are usually outward-facing although occasionally stem-clasping. In several hostas these are showy, and if the true leaves are variegated, the bracts will be similarly variegated.

The raceme may be dense or sparse. The flowers are usually disposed to one side, but may be disposed all around the scape. Hosta flowers last only a day.

Hosta Cultivation

In broad terms, hostas need a fertile soil that is moist but well drained, a measure of protection against the heat of the sun, and shelter from strong winds. They are well adapted to cultivation throughout the temperate world, are reliably frost tolerant to about 28°F (−2°C) and can tolerate summer temperatures as high as 100°F (38°C) for short times. While in active growth, hostas require about 1 in. (25 mm) of water per week. They are very tolerant of drought (though do not look good when droughted) and temporary flooding.

What to Look for When Buying Hostas

When buying a hosta, look for healthy leaves and healthy roots. The leaves should be turgid, of good color; they should not show signs of any physical damage. The roots should be plump and

A dense cluster of opening buds of *Hosta* 'Deep Blue Sea'.

The long-tubed flowers of *Hosta plantaginea*.

Hosta 'Halcyon' at the Royal Horticultural Society's Garden, Wisley, England, holds its color well into late summer when given good light to dappled shade.

white, and they should be plentiful enough to bind the soil without filling the pot or encircling the bottom of the pot. If the soil falls away from the roots, the plant has not been in the pot long enough, and if the roots fill too much of the pot, it has probably been in the pot too long.

Reject any hosta that has poor, mainly brown roots or any sign of damage to the roots. Particular care should be taken when buying tissue-cultured plants, as these are not always adequately weaned.

When to Plant

Hostas should be planted when the soil is open and workable. In a mild, maritime climate, this can be any time from mild spells in the depths of winter to damp periods in high summer. In warmer climates the planting season is usually late spring. Planting at these times enables the hostas to establish themselves before both the heat and drought of summer and after the frosts of winter.

The hostas should be actively making new roots. This is usually when the first flush of leaves have hardened off but before the second flush,

and at least six weeks before the date of the first killing frost. This gives them time to settle in while the ground is still warm, and it gives the ground time to firm up before the frosts.

Preparing the Ground

The single most important factor in the success of any plant is the thorough prior preparation of the ground. No amount of watering and feeding after planting will make up for poor soil preparation. Most garden soils can be improved by adding organic matter such as peat or coir, finely chopped bark, farmyard manure or good garden compost. Coarse grit should also be added to clays and other heavy soils.

If only one hosta is to be planted, then dig a hole proportional to the expected final size of the hosta. For large hostas, the hole should be a minimum of 3 ft. (90 cm) in diameter, possibly as much as 5 ft. (150 cm). Since hostas are not deep rooting, the hole need be no more than 18 in. (45 cm) deep, but it is important to loosen the soil at the bottom of the hole. The hole should then be back-filled with alternating 2¾ in. (7 cm) layers of soil and organic matter. Each layer

Hosta 'Sun Power', *H.* 'Fortunei Aureomarginata', and *H.* 'Fringe Benefit' with a background of ancient stone walls at the Old Kennels, Nunwick, near Hadrian's Wall in Northumberland, England.

should be thoroughly mixed with the previous layers and then well firmed with the feet.

Where larger numbers of hostas are to be planted, it is simpler to prepare the whole area, either by double-digging or with a mechanical tiller (rotovator). The area should then be covered with 2½ to 4 in. (6 to 10 cm) of organic matter and a scattering of balanced, general fertilizer, then tilled again. On all except sandy or gravelly soils, about 1 in. (2.5 cm) of coarse grit or pea shingle should be spread over the area, and this too should be tilled into the ground. The planting area or the individual holes should be left to settle for several weeks before planting begins.

At planting time, dig a hole in the prepared ground large enough to take all the hosta roots, well spread out. Then make a small mound in the middle of the hole so that the crown of the hosta rests on the apex with the roots running downhill. The roots should be teased out and spread over the sides of the mound. This is particularly important with pot-grown hostas whose roots may be congested. Then return the soil to the hole, firming it with hands or feet. Finally, water the hosta thoroughly. The soil around the hosta

should be mulched to keep the roots cool and prevent water loss through its surface.

Watering

Hostas need a sufficient and regular supply of water during the growing season. Overhead watering can lead to water lying on the leaves, which can in turn cause them to rot, become the focus of fungal infections and attract slugs and snails. It can also destroy the glaucous waxy coating on blue-leaved hostas leaving the leaves dark green. Fine mist sprays can leave unsightly chalky or other discolorations. Water is best applied directly to the roots, beneath the leaves, using a watering can without a rose (perforated nozzle), a watering wand attached to a hose, or a hose that is left trickling slowly for several hours. Seep hoses can be looped around clumps of hostas. Watering is best done in early morning. Watering in the evening and at night encourages slugs and snails.

The same watering principles apply to hostas in containers. These will need to be watered at least every two to three days from the time the leaves emerge in spring until they die down in the autumn. Very large hostas, especially those growing

An island bed of hostas in the garden of Marcia Niswonger, Piqua, Ohio.

in sun, will need as much as 3 gallons (12 liters) of water every day, while hostas of average size will need at least 1 gallon (4.5 liters) a day.

Feeding and Mulching

Hostas only achieve their potential if, in addition to water, they also receive plenty of nourishment. Organic feeds such as farmyard manure, garden compost, or leaf-mold are much advocated, but their nutritional value is always unbalanced and often negligible. It is better to use artificial fertilizers whose nutritional values are known in conjunction with organic mulches.

Ideally, hostas should be lightly mulched in spring and autumn, and fed in spring and early summer. Any heavy fertilization after midsummer promotes soft, sappy growth to be enjoyed by slugs and snails. Farmyard manure, peat, coir, cocoa shells, garden compost, grape waste, shredded bark, crushed corncobs, pine needles, seaweed, and salt hay are all suitable. Organic materials eventually decompose and contribute to the humus level in the soil, but inorganic

mulches such as stones or gravel do not confer this benefit, nor do plastic or woven materials used to suppress weeds.

Where hostas have been planted singly, the mulch should be applied in a ring around the hosta, taking care not to bury the crown as this might cause it to rot in the winter. The mulch should be spread up to or beyond the circumference of the leaf mound. While most hostas are completely frost hardy, it is sometimes expedient to cover the crowns lightly in winter with straw, dry fern fronds, or salt hay to prevent heaving in alternating spells of cold and warmth. The mulch should not be too thick; a depth of no more than 1 in. (2.5 cm) for large hostas and ¼ in. (5 mm) for small hostas is usually sufficient.

Where hostas are planted in groups, the mulch should be spread over the whole area, again avoiding the crowns. The petioles should not be covered as this can be a cause of fungal diseases, especially southern stem blight. Mulches laid too thickly will create nesting sites for voles and other rodents.

Growing in Containers

The first essential is that the containers are large enough to take the roots with room to spare for two or three years of further growth. The containers should have large enough holes in the bottom to ensure good drainage, but the holes themselves should be covered with crocks (pieces of broken terracotta pots or roof tiles), wire screening, or porous matting so that the growing mix does not slip through them. In general, medium to large and very large hostas are best grown in a soil-based growing mix, though medium and small or miniature hostas do better in soilless potting mixes with coarse grit added.

Because container-grown hostas require so much watering, soil nutrients are soon leached out and need replacing. With very large hostas, it helps to put a layer of organic manure over the crocks and then to mix some organic manure in with the growing mix. Some growing mixes contain fertilizer, but usually only sufficient for a few

Container-grown hostas are arranged at varying heights in the Pat and George Raeder garden, adding interest to the ground-level plants.

weeks. Slow-release fertilizer granules or pellets should then be scattered on the growing mix under the leaves once or twice in the growing season and never after midsummer. An alternative is a weekly, dilute foliar feed, but again not after midsummer.

Any healthy hosta will eventually need to be moved on to a larger container or split and put back in the same pot but in fresh growing mix. If this is not done, the leaves will diminish in size and may become misshapen.

Pests, Diseases, and Other Threats to Hostas

The best defenses against the pests and diseases of hostas are to grow healthy, vigorous plants, to grow them in optimum conditions, and to be vigilant in checking so that pests and diseases can be dealt with using a minimum of chemicals.

Slugs and Snails

Slugs and snails are notoriously the most troublesome pests of hostas. Slugs remain active throughout the whole year. Snails, by contrast, become inactive at the onset of cold weather.

The most effective way of reducing slug and snail populations in most gardens is to go out at night with a light and collect these pests in a container that is suitable for destruction. Slug baits are most successful when applied on mild evenings, particularly in warm weather in spring. Salt, borax, and ammonia act as contact poisons when applied directly onto the slug or snail and their eggs. A 10-percent solution of household ammonia can be a useful preventative when applied to the crown and nearby area as shoots first emerge in the spring.

Barriers are an alternative to poisons since slugs and snails avoid sharp, hairy, or very absorbent surfaces. Among materials that deter because of their sharpness are sand, coarse grit, sharp cinders, wood ashes, diatomaceous earth, broken eggshells, and crushed oyster and scallop shells. Other types of barriers, such as continuous strips or tapes of copper or aluminum placed around the hostas, cause a chemical reaction

With their wide margin, the spectacular leaves of *Hosta* 'Liberty' brighten up a moderately shaded site.

hermaphrodita is most effective when applied in spring. It also works best on light sandy soils rather than on heavy clays. It only destroys slugs, not snails.

An additional measure of control can be achieved by removing dead and dying leaves and not allowing decaying vegetation to build up in the garden. Hosta leaves should be removed as soon as they start to turn yellow or show signs of decay.

Other garden rubbish should be kept to a minimum. Bricks or planks of wood, for example, provide ideal breeding sites. The continual cultivation of the soil's surface can also keep slug and snail populations down by exposing their eggs to the air.

Vine Weevils

Vine weevils (*Otiorhynchus sulcatus*), sometimes called black vine weevils to distinguish them from clay-colored weevils, are fat, creamy white, C-shaped, legless grubs about ½ in. (1 cm) long that have tiny heads of a malicious shade of burnt sienna. They feed on the roots of hostas, causing the leaves to turn yellow and the plant to wilt and usually die.

Vine weevils are often more of a problem in pots than in the open ground, and once they become established they can be difficult to eradicate completely. A parasitic nematode, *Heterorhabditis megidis*, provides the most effective control. It is usually bought by mail order and is applied to the soil through a watering can. Adult vine weevils can also be trapped, especially under glass or in tunnels, by placing rolls of corrugated paper, old sacking or canvas on or near the ground to provide daytime refuge for the weevils. These materials should be inspected daily and shaken out over a clean surface where the weevils can be spotted and destroyed. The adults can be seen quite easily by torchlight after dark, picked off the plants, and destroyed.

The best mitigation for vine weevils is to kill the larvae, that is, their grubs. The chemical imidacloprid is available in the United Kingdom as a

which makes the slugs and snails overproduce mucilage resulting in their desiccation.

Where hostas are growing in containers, slugs and snails can be deterred if the containers are raised off the ground on small feet and if a band of petroleum jelly or fruit-tree grease is placed around the outside of the container. Penetrating oils act as deterrents if they are sprayed on the outsides of containers. Copper tape tied round the outside of pots will also deter slugs and snails.

The ultimate controls are biological ones. The pathogenic nematode *Phasmarhabditis*

Hosta 'Daybreak' in the foreground of a lush planting of hostas and other foliage in Gil Jones's garden.

packet specifically marketed for vine weevil control. In the United States and some other countries, it is marketed as an insecticide for the white grubs of Japanese beetles in lawns and gardens. It is available as both a granule and liquid, and is easily spread or sprayed onto hosta beds as well as containers.

Foliar Nematodes

Foliar nematodes (*Aphelenchoides fragariae* and *Ditylenchus dipsaci*) can cause severe damage to hostas and are spread by splashing water. They overwinter in the crowns of hostas, migrating in the spring to the leaf blades, where they feed and multiply between the veins, causing the characteristic interveinal browning, which often is not apparent until midsummer or later. Remov-

ing affected foliage may limit the infestation but will not be a complete remedy. Individual divisions of mildly infested plants should be soaked in water held at a temperature of 120°F (49°C) for 15 to 20 minutes, after which they should be potted up and grown on in isolation from other hostas for at least six months.

Deer

Deer can be a considerable problem in rural areas, chewing hostas right down to the ground. The traditional wisdom is that barriers are only effective when they are over 8 ft. (240 cm) tall. Where space permits, a sequence of lower barriers is effective, especially if they are too close together for the deer to gather themselves to spring over the next one.

HOSTAS FOR SPECIFIC PURPOSES AND LOCATIONS

The lists that follow are representative only and do not include every hosta described in this guide.

Hostas with Green Leaves

Hostas with plain green leaves must have very special qualities to capture the interest of modern hosta growers. Among these qualities are unusual surface texture, interesting leaf shape or plant habit, heavy racemes of flower, intensely white leaf backs, or outstanding red petioles and scapes.

H. 'Betsy King'
H. 'Bridegroom'
H. 'Cinnamon Sticks'
H. 'Corkscrew'
H. 'Cutting Edge'
H. 'Devon Green'
H. 'Glacier Cascade'
H. 'Green Fountain'
H. 'Harry van der Laar'
H. 'Invincible'
H. 'Jade Cascade'
H. 'Joseph'
H. 'Komodo Dragon'
H. 'Lakeside Black Satin'
H. 'Lakeside Lollipop'
H. longissima
H. 'Marilyn Monroe'
H. 'Niagara Falls'
H. 'One Man's Treasure'
H. plantaginea
H. 'Potomac Pride'
H. rectifolia
H. 'Royal Standard'
H. 'T Rex'
H. 'Tardiflora'
H. ventricosa
H. venusta
H. 'Yakushima Mizu'
H. yingeri

Hostas with Chartreuse, Yellow, or Gold Leaves

Yellowness in hosta leaves signifies the absence of chlorophyll. Viridescent hostas produce more chlorophyll as temperatures rise, lutescent hostas produce less. Knowing whether a hosta is viridescent or lutescent can be a useful guide in placing it in the garden: lutescent hostas need more sunlight than viridescent hostas to bring out their coloring to its fullest. The brightest lemon to golden yellows will light up dark areas of the garden and will actually draw the eye to that spot. Do not overuse yellow, however, as too many individual, yellow-leaved hostas scattered over a border among darker shades can produce a spotty, inharmonious effect and can appear agitating in an otherwise restful garden. Yellow hostas, if planted sensitively, will blend in well with hostas of other colors, especially blues, grays, and those with gold margins. The yellow leaves that are particularly sensitive to strong sunlight are at their most vulnerable early in the season when the leaves are expanding. Such hostas need temporary shade if they put on their leaves before the trees.

H. 'August Moon' (lutescent)
H. 'Chartreuse Wiggles' (lutescent)
H. 'Cheatin Heart' (lutescent)
H. 'Dawn's Early Light' (viridescent)
H. 'Daybreak' (lutescent)
H. 'Dragon Tails' (lutescent)
H. 'English Sunrise' (viridescent)
H. 'Fire Island' (viridescent)
H. 'Fort Knox' (lutescent)
H. 'Gold Edger' (viridescent)
H. 'Gold Regal' (lutescent)
H. 'Golden Sculpture' (lutescent)
H. 'Golden Teacup' (viridescent)

Opposite: Hosta sieboldii 'First Mate' (right middle) with *H.* 'Chantilly Lace' (top center) and miniature *H.* 'Bitsy Gold' (bottom right).

H. 'Great Lakes Gold' (lutescent)
H. 'Jimmy Crack Corn' (lutescent)
H. 'King Tut' (lutescent)
H. 'Krugerrand' (lutescent)
H. 'Little Black Scape' (lutescent)
H. 'Maui Buttercups' (lutescent)
H. 'Midas Touch' (lutescent)
H. 'Miki' (lutescent)
H. 'Piedmont Gold' (lutescent)
H. 'Sum and Substance' (lutescent)
H. 'Sun Power' (lutescent)
H. 'Zounds' (lutescent)

Hostas with Very Blue Leaves

Listed here are those hostas which appear, due to their heavy glaucous bloom, to have really blue leaves at midsummer, not blue-green or green-gray. Most will assume a blue-green tinge earlier or later in the growing season, but some will remain almost blue until autumn. This phenomenon depends on genetic make-up, light levels, and degree of summer heat.

H. 'Abiqua Drinking Gourd'
H. 'Azure Snow'
H. 'Big Daddy'
H. 'Blue Hawaii'
H. 'Blue Jay'
H. 'Brother Ronald'
H. 'Buckshaw Blue'
H. 'Camelot'
H. 'Deep Blue Sea'
H. 'Dorset Blue'
H. 'Hadspen Blue'
H. 'Love Pat'
H. 'Powder Blue'
H. 'Prairie Sky'
H. sieboldiana 'Elegans'
H. 'Silver Bay'
H. 'Ultramarine'
H. 'Winfield Blue'

Hostas with Blue-Gray Leaves

These hostas are best used near the house, either as container specimens or planted to set off stonework or paving. Their grayish blue leaves are due either to the basic leaf color or sometimes to the denseness of a glaucous gray bloom on a blue leaf. The latter group of plants can quickly lose their bloom if exposed to hot sun, leaving a shiny or blotched surface on the leaves.

H. 'Baby Bunting'
H. 'Blue Angel'
H. 'Blue Sliver'
H. 'Bold Ruffles'
H. 'Great Plains'
H. 'Gunsmoke'
H. 'Krossa Regal'
H. 'Metallic Sheen'
H. 'Mississippi Delta'
H. 'Pewterware'
H. 'Popo'
H. 'Queen of the Seas'
H. 'Quilted Skies'

Hostas with Blue-Green Leaves

This category embraces hostas that are not blue enough to belong in the blue section and yet are definitely too blue to belong in the green section. Many leaves unfurl green, turn blue for a few weeks, and finally take on greenish tints; others start blue but hold this for a very short time before becoming greener.

H. 'Andrew Jackson'
H. 'Big Mama'
H. 'Bigfoot'
H. 'Blue Arrow'
H. 'Blue Boy'
H. 'Blue Cadet'
H. 'Blue Mouse Ears'
H. 'Deane's Dream'
H. 'Lederhosen'
H. 'Metallica'
H. 'Millenium'
H. nigrescens
H. 'Osprey'
H. 'Salute'
H. 'Sea Lotus Leaf'
H. 'Silvery Slugproof'
H. 'Tutu'
H. 'Wheaton Blue'

Hostas with Gray-Green Leaves

Unlike the blue-gray hostas which have a thick glaucous bloom on their leaves, hostas in this category often have a thin bloom. In some cases, the bloom disappears rapidly, even on plants growing in shade, and their distinctive grayness gives way to green. Some hostas with outstanding gray-green leaves look best when grown in naturalistic plantings or on the waterside.

H. 'Abiqua Ground Cover'
H. 'Big John'
H. 'Cutting Edge'
H. 'Fortunei Hyacinthina'
H. 'Phantom'
H. 'Pineapple Poll'
H. 'Prince of Wales'
H. 'Quilted Hearts'
H. 'Red October'
H. 'Snowden'

Hostas with Marginally Variegated Leaves

Marginally variegated hostas are those whose variegation is in the margin of the leaf. The leaf center is darker in color than the margin.

H. 'Afternoon Delight'
H. 'Alex Summers'
H. 'Alvatine Taylor'
H. 'American Dream'
H. 'American Eagle'
H. 'American Icon'
H. 'Arc de Triomphe'
H. 'Atlantis'
H. 'Band of Gold'
H. 'Blazing Saddles'
H. 'Blue Flame'
H. 'Blue River'
H. 'Bob Olson'
H. 'Candy Cane'
H. 'Carnival'
H. 'Carolina Sunshine'
H. 'Christmas Tree'
H. 'Climax'
H. 'Crepe Suzette'
H. 'Crispula'
H. 'Dark Star'

H. 'Deja Blu'
H. 'Diana Remembered'
H. 'Eagle's Nest'
H. 'Earth Angel'
H. 'El Capitan'
H. 'El Niño'
H. 'Electrum Stater'
H. 'Emily Dickinson'
H. 'Fantabulous'
H. 'Fragrant Bouquet'
H. 'Frosted Jade'
H. 'Frozen Margarita'
H. 'Golden Tiara'
H. 'Great River Sonata'
H. 'Harpoon'
H. 'Independence'
H. 'Jack of Diamonds'
H. 'Key Lime Pie'
H. 'Lakeside Dragonfly'
H. 'Lakeside Kaleidoscope'
H. 'Leading Lady'
H. 'Magic Fire'
H. 'Mardi Gras'
H. 'Memories of Dorothy'
H. 'Mildred Seaver'
H. montana 'Aureomarginata'
H. 'Mount Tom'
H. 'Mourning Dove'
H. 'Opipara Bill Brincka'
H. 'Ops'
H. 'Patriot'
H. 'Pilgrim'
H. 'Queen Josephine'
H. 'Regal Splendor'
H. 'Sagae'
H. 'Satisfaction'
H. 'Sergeant Pepper'
H. 'Shazaam'
H. sieboldiana 'American Halo'
H. sieboldiana 'Frances Williams'
H. sieboldiana 'Northern Exposure'
H. 'So Sweet'
H. 'Stiletto'
H. 'Tambourine'
H. 'Unforgettable'
H. 'Wide Brim'
H. 'Wolverine'
H. 'Woolly Mammoth'

Hostas with Medio-Variegated Leaves

Medio-variegated hostas are those whose variegation is at the center rather than on the margin. Since the 1990s they have become by far the most popular. However, they are usually not as vigorous as hostas with marginal variegation because so much of the central portion of the leaf blade lacks sufficient chlorophyll to enable the plants to thrive. Many blue-margined, medio-variegated hostas unfurl with only midgreen color and do not assume their expected variegation for several weeks. They must be divided approximately every few years to retain the most pleasing balance between variegation and leaf base color.

H. 'Allegan Fog'
H. 'American Sweetheart'
H. 'Ani Machi'
H. 'Brenda's Beauty'
H. 'Brother Stephan'
H. 'Captain Kirk'
H. 'Cascades'
H. 'Cathedral Windows'
H. 'Cat's Eye'
H. 'Chinese Sunrise'
H. 'Cornbelt'
H. 'Cracker Crumbs'
H. 'Dancing in the Rain'
H. 'Emerald Ruff Cut'
H. 'Emerald Tiara'
H. 'Fire and Ice'
H. 'Gold Standard'
H. 'Guardian Angel'
H. 'Hanky Panky'
H. 'High Society'
H. 'Holy Molé'
H. 'Inniswood'
H. 'June'
H. 'Kiwi Full Monty'
H. 'Lakeside Love Affaire'
H. 'Lakeside Shore Master'
H. 'Little Caesar'
H. 'Little Sunspot'
H. 'Lonesome Dove'
H. 'Night Before Christmas'
H. 'Olive Branch'
H. 'Pandora's Box'

H. 'Paradigm'
H. 'Paradise Joyce'
H. 'Paul's Glory'
H. 'Peanut'
H. 'Pole Cat'
H. 'Red Hot Flash'
H. 'Revolution'
H. *sieboldiana* 'Borwick Beauty'
H. *sieboldiana* 'Dream Weaver'
H. *sieboldiana* 'Eskimo Pie'
H. *sieboldii* 'First Mate'
H. 'Striptease'
H. 'Summer Music'
H. 'Warpaint'
H. 'Whirlwind'
H. 'Xanadu'

Hostas for Flower Arrangements

H. 'Bold Ruffles'
H. 'Cornbelt'
H. 'Cutting Edge'
H. 'Fortunei Aureomarginata'
H. 'June'
H. 'Krossa Regal'
H. *longissima*
H. 'Niagara Falls'
H. 'Pilgrim'
H. *sieboldiana* 'Elegans'
H. *sieboldiana* 'Frances Williams'
H. *sieboldiana* 'Great Arrival'
H. 'Tutu'
H. 'Wide Brim'

Sun-Tolerant Hostas

H. 'August Moon'
H. 'Carolina Sunshine'
H. 'Cathedral Windows'
H. 'Dee's Golden Jewel'
H. 'Eagle's Nest'
H. 'Fortunei Aureomarginata'
H. 'Fragrant Bouquet'
H. 'Gentle Giant'
H. 'Guacamole'
H. 'Lady Isobel Barnett'
H. *plantaginea*
H. 'Sum and Substance'
H. 'Sweet Innocence'
H. 'Yesterday's Memories'

Hostas for Southern Gardens

Shade is essential for this group.

H. 'Alex Summers'
H. 'Alvatine Taylor'
H. 'Atlantis'
H. 'Blue Angel'
H. 'Carolina Sunshine'
H. 'Chartreuse Wiggles'
H. 'Daybreak'
H. 'Frosted Jade'
H. 'Golden Tiara'
H. 'Guacamole'
H. 'Holy Molé'
H. 'Jade Cascade'
H. 'Krossa Regal'
H. 'Lakeside Shore Master'
H. 'Little Sunspot'
H. 'Patriot'
H. 'Piedmont Gold'
H. plantaginea and forms
H. 'Red Hot Flash'
H. 'Satisfaction'
H. 'So Sweet'
H. 'Stiletto'
H. 'Sum and Substance'
H. yingeri

Easy-to-Grow Miniature Hostas

H. 'Baby Bunting'
H. 'Blue Mouse Ears'
H. 'Cracker Crumbs'
H. 'Pandora's Box'
H. 'Peanut'
H. 'Popo'
H. venusta

Hostas with Outstanding Flowers

H. 'Blue Mouse Ears'
H. 'Cathedral Windows'
H. 'Diana Remembered'
H. 'Fragrant Bouquet'
H. 'Frozen Margarita'
H. 'Green Fountain'
H. 'Guacamole'
H. 'Holy Molé'
H. 'One Man's Treasure'
H. plantaginea and forms

H. 'Red October'
H. 'Royal Standard'
H. ventricosa and forms

Hostas for Edging

H. 'Baby Bunting'
H. 'Blond Elf'
H. 'Blue Boy'
H. 'Candy Cane'
H. 'Chartreuse Wiggles'
H. 'Chinese Sunrise'
H. 'Diamond Tiara'
H. 'Ginko Craig'
H. 'Gold Edger'
H. sieboldii 'First Mate'
H. 'Stiletto'

Hostas for Ground Cover

H. 'Abiqua Ground Cover'
H. 'Blue Boy'
H. 'Dark Star'
H. 'Pearl Lake'
H. 'Resonance'
H. 'Stiletto'
H. 'Tambourine'
H. 'Whirlwind'

Hostas for Rock Gardens

H. 'Blue Mouse Ears'
H. 'Cat's Eyes'
H. 'Cheatin Heart'
H. 'Cracker Crumbs'
H. 'Dragon Tails'
H. 'Popo'
H. venusta
H. 'Yakusima Mizu'

Slug-Resistant Hostas

H. 'American Eagle'
H. 'Dick Ward'
H. 'Great Lakes Gold'
H. 'Invincible'
H. 'Krossa Regal'
H. 'Powder Blue'
H. sieboldiana cultivars
H. 'Silvery Slugproof'
H. 'Zounds'

Hosta 'Abiqua Drinking Gourd'

Medium to large, very blue leaves.

Clump size & habit: 36 in. wide × 20 in. high (90 × 50 cm). An open mound.

Description: Leaf blade 8½ × 8½ in. (21 × 21 cm), of thick substance, rich dark blue, strongly seersuckered and puckered, deeply cupped, edge flat, nearly round with tapered, overlapping lobes. Petiole stout, gray-blue. Flower near-white on an upright, leafy, gray-blue, 22 in. (55 cm) scape in midsummer; fertile.

Comments: Avoid planting under trees where the leaves can collect falling debris. Needs good light and protection from strong wind. The leaf can cup 4 in. (10 cm), revealing the powdery gray underside.

Similar: *H.* 'Blue Canoe' (leaves longer and not holding the blue color as well).

Hosta 'Abiqua Ground Cover'

Small, gray-green leaves.

Clump size & habit: 12 in. wide × 9 in. high (30 × 23 cm). A rhizomatous mound.

Description: Leaf blade 2½ × 2 in. (6 × 5 cm), of average substance, smooth, gray-green, widely veined, edge slightly undulate, widely oval with slightly folded, heart-shaped pinched lobes. Petiole light gray-green. Flower bell-shaped, lavender, on an upright or leaning, leafy, glaucous gray-green, 15 in. (38 cm) scape in high summer; fertile.

Comments: Provide two hours of morning sun in cooler climates, good light or moderate shade all day in warmer climates. Vigorous, fast growing. Makes a superb groundcover, although it does not form dense mounds.

Hosta 'Abiqua Recluse'

Medium to large, yellowish leaves.

Clump size & habit: 36 in. wide × 18 in. high (90 × 45 cm). An unruly mound.

Description: Leaf blade 12¾ × 9 in. (32 × 23 cm), of thick substance, metallic golden yellow, shiny above and thinly glaucous below, lightly seersuckered, veins ribbed, edge almost flat, cupped or convex, oval with heart-shaped pinched to overlapping lobes. Petiole pale chartreuse-yellow. Flower palest lavender to near-white on an upright, leafy, chartreuse, 20 in. (50 cm) scape in late summer; fertile.

Hosta 'Abiqua Drinking Gourd'

Hosta 'Abiqua Ground Cover'

Opposite: Mature hostas in the garden of Patsy Stygall in Indianapolis, Indiana: *Hosta* 'Cascades' (lower right) with *H.* 'Blue Blazes' (center) and *H.* 'Nancy Minks' (lower left).

Hosta 'Abiqua Recluse'

Hosta 'Afternoon Delight' in foreground

Hosta 'Alex Summers'

Comments: Needs some sun for best color. Provide afternoon shade in hot climates. Slow to moderate growth rate. Pest resistant.

Similar: *H.* 'Abiqua Gold Shield' (leaves less rounded), **H.* 'August Moon' (flowers three weeks later than the yellow-leaved selections of *H. sieboldiana*), *H.* 'City Lights' and *H.* 'Radiance' (leaves intensely seersuckered), *H.* 'Faith', **H.* 'Golden Sculpture', *H.* 'White Vision' (leaves yellow with a green midrib),**H.* 'Zounds'.

Sports: **H.* 'Electrum Stater', *H.* 'Wooden Nickel' (leaves green with a yellow margin).

Hosta 'Afternoon Delight'

Large, marginally variegated leaves.

Clump size & habit: 47 in. wide × 24 in. high (117 × 60 cm). An upright, spreading mound.

Description: Leaf blade 12 × 8 in. (30 × 20 cm), of thick substance, dark green, widely margined rich gold, matt above and glaucous below, seersuckered, mostly convex, edge undulate, broadly oval with open to pinched heart-shaped lobes. Petiole chartreuse, outlined in green. Flower pale lavender on an upright, bare, glaucous yellow, 32 in. (80 cm) scape in midsummer; fertile.

Comments: Leaf margin turns brighter gold in some morning sun. Slow to moderate growth rate. Reasonably pest resistant.

Similar: *H.* 'Tyler's Treasure'.

Hosta 'Alex Summers'

Large, marginally variegated leaves.

Clump size & habit: 60 in. wide × 32 in. high (150 × 80 cm). A striking, vase-shaped mound.

Description: Leaf blade 9 × 7½ in. (23 × 19 cm), of thick substance, midgreen, very widely margined chartreuse turning creamy yellow streaked chartreuse, dimpled, closely veined, edge slightly wavy, slightly dished, oval with a pointed tip and heart-shaped open to pinched lobes. Petiole stout, leaning, glaucous green, outlined in cream. Flower large, bell-shaped, grayish mauve, on a stout, leafy, upright, glaucous green, 30–39 in. (75–98 cm) scape in midsummer; fertile.

Comments: Morning sun in cooler climates will intensify leaf color which will remain muted in deep shade. Moderate growth rate.

Similar: *H.* 'David Reath', *H.* 'Independence Day' (leaf margin narrower and more muted in color).

Hosta 'Allegan Fog'

Medium, medio-variegated leaves.

Clump size & habit: 18 in. wide × 13 in. high (45 × 33 cm). A compact mound.

Description: Leaf blade 4¾ × 3 in. (12 × 8 cm), of thin substance, greenish white becoming finely flecked dark green, irregularly margined dark green, matt above and glaucous below, edge slightly rippled, twisted, arching, widely lanceolate with a long, curved tip and tapered, open lobes. Petiole narrowly channeled, white, outlined in dark green. Flower purple-streaked lavender on an upright, leafy, glaucous green, 41 in. (102 cm) scape in mid to high summer; barely fertile.

Comments: Viridescent. The central variegation is stippled and flecked olive green and slowly fades. Light to moderate shade. Careful positioning is important for best color. Vigorous, fast growing. Divide frequently.

Similar: *H.* 'Alley Oop' (habit smaller).

Hosta 'Alligator Shoes'

Medium, marginally variegated leaves.

Clump size & habit: 24 in. wide × 18 in. high (60 × 45 cm). A well-poised mound.

Description: Leaf blade 7½ × 5 in. (19 × 13 cm), of thick substance, blue-green to olive green, irregularly and narrowly margined cream to white with random gray-green streaks, matt above and glaucous below, closely seersuckered, edge unevenly rippled, arching, convex, widely oval with a twisted tip and heart-shaped open lobes. Petiole shallowly channeled, gray-green. Flower palest lavender on a leaning, leafy, green, 36 in. (90 cm) scape from mid to late summer; fertile.

Comments: Grows better in morning sun. Moderate growth rate. Pest resistant. The rough, pebbled texture gives great personality.

Hosta 'Allegan Fog'

Hosta 'Alligator Shoes'

Hosta 'Alvatine Taylor'

Large, marginally variegated leaves.

Clump size & habit: 48 in. wide × 30 in. high (120 × 75 cm). A colorful, dense mound.

Description: Leaf blade 9–10 × 7–8½ in. (23–25 × 18–21 cm), of thick substance, glaucous blue-gray, widely and irregularly margined muted golden yellow, prominently veined, seersuckered and puckered, edge slightly undulate, widely oval with heart-shaped rounded to flat lobes. Petiole stout, light green, faintly outlined in yellow. Flower white on an upright, leafy, glaucous green, 32 in. (80 cm) scape in high summer; fertile.

Hosta 'Alvatine Taylor'

Hosta 'American Dream'

Hosta 'American Eagle'

Comments: Tolerates morning sun in cooler climates. Slow to moderate growth rate. Pest resistant. Leaf surface develops an attractive sheen by summer's end. Winner of the 1998 Alex J. Summers Distinguished Merit Hosta Award.

Similar: *H.* 'Abiqua Moonbeam' (leaves shorter, more brightly colored).

Sports: *H.* 'Doubloons' (leaves bright golden with a metallic cast).

Hosta 'American Dream'

Large, marginally variegated leaves.

Clump size & habit: 41 in. wide × 24 in. high (102 × 60 cm). A dense, upright mound.

Description: Leaf blade 10 × 7½ in. (25 × 19 cm), of good substance, chartreuse turning golden creamy yellow, irregularly margined white and streaked chartreuse, matt above and thinly glaucous below, seersuckered, edge slightly rippled, cupped or convex, widely oval with heart-shaped folded lobes. Petiole chartreuse, outlined in ivory. Flower lavender on an upright, leafy, chartreuse, 18¾ in. (47 cm) scape in late summer; fertile.

Comments: Provide morning sun in cooler climates. Strong but slow growing. The variegated margin can be up to 2¾ in. (7 cm) wide.

Similar: *H.* 'Lakeside Cha Cha', *H.* 'Sea Dream', *H.* 'Sunshine Glory', *H.* 'Zodiac'.

Hosta 'American Eagle'

Large, marginally variegated leaves.

Clump size & habit: 30 in. wide × 20 in. high (75 × 50 cm). An upright mound.

Description: Leaf blade 9 × 8½ in. (23 × 21 cm), of thick substance, dark green, widely and irregularly margined golden yellow streaked chartreuse, matt above and glaucous below, seersuckered, edge almost flat, shallowly dished, nearly round with heart-shaped pinched lobes. Petiole dark green, finely outlined in creamy yellow. Flower pale lavender on an upright, chartreuse, leafy, 30 in. (75 cm) scape in mid to high summer; fertile.

Comments: Provide some morning sun in cooler climates. Slow growing. Pest resistant. The broad margin is in striking contrast to the exceptionally dark green leaves. Outstanding.

Similar: *H.* 'Laura and Darrell' (leaf underside strongly veined).

Hosta 'American Icon'

Large, marginally variegated leaves.

Clump size & habit: 63 in. wide × 22½ in. high (157 × 56 cm). A spectacular, arching mound.

Description: Leaf blade 12 × 8 in. (30 × 20 cm), of average substance, matt mid to dark green, very widely and irregularly margined bright

Hosta 'American Icon'

golden yellow with feathering into the green center, veins deeply impressed, dimpled, edge very ruffled, arching, oval with a pointed tip and heart-shaped pinched lobes. Petiole dark green, outlined in yellow. Flower palest lavender to near-white on an upright, leafy, dark green, 30 in. (75 cm) scape from early to midsummer; fertile.

Comments: Site in moderate shade to enhance the dramatic contrast between the margin and the leaf center. Good growth rate. Differs from its yellow-leaved parent *H.* 'Choo Choo Train' in having a green leaf center. A superb specimen plant.

Hosta 'American Sweetheart'
Medium to large, medio-variegated leaves.

Clump size & habit: 24½ in. wide × 20½ in. high (61 × 51 cm). A tight, upright mound.

Description: Leaf blade 9 × 7 in. (23 × 18 cm), of good substance, chartreuse turning white, very widely and irregularly margined dark olive green with chartreuse streaking, satiny above and shiny below, veins closely ribbed, edge flat, broadly oval with a pointed tip and rounded pinched to folded lobes. Petiole ivory, with red dots, outlined in green. Flower pale lavender on an upright, leafy, ivory, 30 in. (75 cm) scape in late summer; fertility unknown.

Comments: Light shade in hot climates, tolerates some morning sun in cooler climates. Increases slowly. Differs from its parent *H.* 'Sea Thunder' in having thicker leaves with a wider margin and with a central variegation which does not scorch. The flowers are also larger. A superb border specimen. Flourishes in containers if given adequate moisture. Divide frequently.

Similar: *H.* 'Ann Kulpa', *H.* 'Indian Feather', *H.* 'Lakeside Love Affaire', *H.* 'Lakeside Meter Maid', *H.* 'Night Before Christmas'.

Hosta 'Andrew'
Large, medio-variegated leaves.

Clump size & habit: 32 in. wide × 20¾ in. (80 × 52 cm) high. A layered mound of eye-catching foliage.

Hosta 'American Sweetheart' showing signs of reversion.

Description: Leaf blade 9 × 7½ in. (23 × 19 cm), of thick substance, ivory white, very widely and irregularly margined glaucous dark blue-green with paler green streaking, seersuckered, edge kinked towards the base, broadly oval with a recurved tip and heart-shaped pinched lobes. Petiole stout, ivory, finely outlined in blue-green. Flower lavender-striped white, subtended by pinkish ivory bracts outlined in blue-green, on an upright, leafy, 25 in. (63 cm) scape in midsummer; sterile.

Comments: Tolerates morning sun in cooler climates but the bluish margins turn green more quickly than in dappled sunlight to light shade. Worth the effort of finding the most beneficial site to maximize the effect of this wonderful new introduction. An embroidered effect occurs at the junction of the variegation and the margin color. Very slow to increase until the wide margin develops. Pest resistant. Divide frequently.

Similar: *H.* 'American Masterpiece'.

Hosta 'Andrew Jackson'
Large to giant, blue-green leaves.

Clump size & habit: 54 in. wide × 30½ in. high (135 × 76 cm). An upright mound.

Description: Leaf blade 12¾ × 9 in. (32 × 23 cm), very thick, glaucous intense blue-green, seersuckered, edge distinctly rippled, wavy and slightly twisted, deeply folded, oval with rounded pinched lobes. Petiole glaucous pale blue. Flower near-white blushed lavender in a dense raceme on an upright, leafy, glaucous blue-green, 31-½

Hosta 'Andrew'

Hosta 'Andrew Jackson'

in. (79 cm) scape from early to midsummer; fertility unknown.

Comments: Light to full shade. Pest resistant. Zones 3–9.

Similar: *H.* 'Ulysses S. Grant' (leaf edge wavier).

Hosta 'Angel Feathers'

Medium, marginally variegated leaves.

Clump size & habit: 34¾ in. wide × 16¾ in. high (87 × 42 cm). A dense, somewhat upright mound.

Description: Leaf blade 7 × 4½ in. (18 × 11 cm), of thick substance, medium green, widely and irregularly margined golden yellow to creamy white with feathering toward the midrib, satiny above and glaucous below, dimpled, edge widely rippled but flattening with maturity, triangular with a conspicuous tip and round to tapered, pinched lobes. Petiole green, outlined in creamy yellow. Flower pale purple on an upright, leafy, 24 in. (60 cm) scape in midsummer; fertility unknown.

Comments: Provide shade all day. Rapid growth rate. Makes a colorful hosta with attractively shaped leaves.

Hosta 'Ani Machi'

Medium, medio-variegated leaves.

Clump size & habit: 36 in. wide × 18 in. high (90 × 45 cm). An upright, sinuous mound.

Description: Leaf blade 7½ × 3 in. (19 × 8 cm), of average substance, smooth, glossy golden yellow, widely and evenly margined dark olive green with occasional streaking, edge slightly rippled, elliptic to narrowly oval and twisted towards the recurved tip, lobes tapered and open. Petiole shallowly channeled, yellow, outlined in dark green. Flowers light violet on an upright, leafy, green, purple-dotted, 26 in. (65 cm) scape in late summer; fertile.

Comments: Viridescent. Leaf center turns pale green at or before flowering time. Grow in light to moderate shade. Slow growth rate; needs good cultivation and hot summers to

Hosta 'Angel Feathers'

maintain its vigor. Divide frequently. Often incorrectly called *H.* 'Geisha'. Zones 3–9.

Similar: *H.* 'Mary Marie Ann' (leaf variegation paler colored).

Sports: *H.* 'Apple Court' (leaves smaller, more twisted, with a white center).

Hosta 'Ann Kulpa'

Medium to large, medio-variegated leaves.

Clump size & habit: 24 in. wide × 20 in. high (60 × 50 cm). A layered mound.

Description: Leaf blade 8 × 6½ in. (20 × 16 cm), of good substance, satiny, yellow turning ivory white, widely and irregularly margined light green turning dark green, with a blue cast in early summer and gray-green streaks, dimpled, strongly veined, edge flat to slightly undulate, folded, widely oval with heart-shaped pinched lobes. Petiole ivory white, striped dark green. Flower bell-shaped, lavender with translucent edges, on an upright, leafy, ivory white, 28 in. (70 cm) scape from mid to high summer; sterile.

Comments: Grow in morning sun in cooler climates. Vigorous. Moderate growth rate. Divide frequently.

Similar: *H.* 'Captain Kirk'.

Hosta 'Antioch'

Medium to large, marginally variegated leaves.

Clump size & habit: 49 in. wide × 22 in. high (122 × 55 cm). A dense mound.

Description: Leaf blade 10 × 5½ in. (25 × 14 cm), of good substance, mid to dark green, irregularly margined chartreuse turning creamy yellow and finally white, with gray-green streaking, satiny above and thinly glaucous below, strongly veined, arching to the ground, convex, oval with heart-shaped pinched lobes. Petiole dark green, outlined in creamy white. Flower lavender, in a dense raceme, on an upright, leafy, green, 28¾ in. (72 cm) scape in midsummer; low fertility.

Comments: Provide light to moderate shade. Vigorous, fast growing. Emerges late. Well-nourished soil and plenty of moisture will increase the width of variegation. Differs from its parent *H.* 'Fortunei Albomarginata' in having longer, more

Hosta 'Ani Machi'

Hosta 'Ann Kulpa', showing sign of reversion.

Hosta 'Antioch'

pointed leaves with wider variegation. Winner of the 1984 Alex J. Summers Distinguished Merit Hosta Award.

Similar: *H.* 'Moerheim', *H.* 'Rhapsody', *H.* 'Shogun', *H.* 'Silver Crown', *H.* 'Spinners'.

Hosta 'Arc de Triomphe'

Large, marginally variegated leaves.

Clump size & habit: 35 in. wide × 24½ in. high (88 × 61 cm). A graceful upright to arching mound.

Description: Leaf blade 12 × 9 in. (30 × 23 cm), of heavy substance, furrowed veins, some seersuckering, dark grayish green, widely and irregularly margined cream to ivory with occasional streaking, satiny above and glaucous below, edge randomly rippled, slightly convex, oval with a prominent tip and heart-shaped pinched lobes. Petiole green, outlined in ivory. Flower purple-striped lavender on an upright, leafy, 36 in. (90 cm) scape from mid to late summer; fertile.

Comments: Light shade. Use with blue-leaved hostas as a contrast. Slow to increase. Some leaf

edges are upturned showing the distinctly glaucous undersides.

Hosta 'Aristocrat'

Medium, marginally variegated leaves.

Clump size & habit: 16 in. wide × 12 in. high (40 × 30 cm). An open mound.

Description: Leaf blade 7½ × 5½ in. (19 × 14 cm), of thick substance, glaucous, rich blue,

Hosta 'Aristocrat'

Hosta 'Arc de Triomphe'

widely and very irregularly margined creamy white with pale gray streaking, dimpled, strongly veined, edge slightly rippled, slightly cupped, widely oval with heart-shaped overlapping lobes. Petiole blue-green, outlined in cream. Flower bell-shaped, lavender-gray to near-white, on an upright, bare, glaucous gray-blue, 18 in. (45 cm) scape in mid to high summer; fertile.

Comments: Provide morning sun in cooler climates to boost the vigor. Slow to increase but well worth the wait. Water sparingly until the roots are established. An ideal pot or container plant as well as a superb specimen plant for a smaller garden.

Similar: *H.* 'El Niño' (a better performer).

Hosta 'Atlantis'

Giant, marginally variegated leaves.

Clump size & habit: 71 in. wide × 30½ in. high (178 × 76 cm). An open, rippled mound.

Description: Leaf blade 13 × 8 in. (33 × 20 cm), of good substance, midgreen, very widely margined and feathered yellow to cream, matt above and glaucous below, veins deeply fur-

rowed, edge widely undulate, twisted, oval with a recurved tip and flat, open to pinched lobes. Petiole coarse, flattish, green, outlined in cream. Flower pale lavender on a leaning, leafy, 45½ in. (114 cm) scape at midsummer; fertile.

Comments: Thrives in warmer gardens. Site in moderate shade to accentuate the depth of color in the variegation. Differs from its parent *H.* 'Abba Dabba Do' in having leaves of heavier substance with wider margins.

Hosta 'August Moon'

Medium to large, yellowish leaves.

Clump size & habit: 42 in. wide × 20 in. high (105 × 50 cm). A dense, somewhat unsymmetrical mound.

Description: Leaf blade 9 × 8 in. (23 × 20 cm), of thick substance, matt, chartreuse, turning soft yellow then glowing golden yellow, seersuckered and puckered, veins strongly marked, edge slightly undulate, usually slightly convex, widely oval with heart-shaped open to pinched lobes. Petiole chartreuse. Flower large, bell-shaped, soft lavender to near-white, on an upright, leafy,

Hosta 'Atlantis'

Hosta 'August Moon'

glaucous grayish yellow, 32 in. (80 cm) scape in high summer.

Comments: Lutescent. Vigorous, fast growing. Among the first yellow-leaved hostas introduced, but now better known for its many glamorous sports. Grows well in dappled shade in hot climates; elsewhere it colors best in four to five hours of morning sun. Although similar in appearance to many yellow-leaved *H. sieboldiana* types, it flowers three weeks later and increases faster. Zones 3–9.

Sports: *H.* 'Abiqua Moonbeam', *H.* 'Crystal Moon', **H.* 'Gemini Moon', and *H.* 'Indiana Knight' (leaves green with a chartreuse margin); *H.* 'Indiana Moonshine' (leaves a muted yellow with a pale green margin); *H.* 'Lunar Magic', *H.* 'Lunar Orbit', **H.* 'September Sun', and *H.* 'September Surprise' (leaves chartreuse with a green margin).

Hosta 'Azure Snow'
Medium to large, very blue leaves.

Clump size & habit: 30 in. wide × 15 in. high (75 × 38 cm). A low, open mound.

Description: Leaf blade 12¾ × 8 in. (32 × 21 cm), of thick substance, powdery turquoise to pale blue, powdery white below, dimpled, widely veined, edge rippled, shallowly undulate, arching, oval to triangular with heart-shaped to rounded pinched lobes. Petiole narrowly channeled, pale green. Flower lavender on an arching, leafy, mauve, 16¾ in. (42 cm) scape from mid to late summer; fertile.

Comments: Light to full shade all day. Moderate growth rate. Leaves have exceptionally thick, white undersides. Zones 3–9.

Similar: *H.* 'Blue Betty Lou', *H.* 'Maekawa'.

Hosta 'Baby Bunting'
Miniature, blue-gray leaves.

Clump size & habit: 12 in. wide × 7 in. high (30 × 18 cm). A dense, rounded mound.

Description: Leaf blade 3½ × 3½ in. (9 × 9 cm), of thick substance, gray-blue, seersuckered, nearly round with deeply heart-shaped pinched lobes. Petiole narrowly channeled, gray-green. Flower bell-shaped, pale lavender, on a leaning, bare, green, 18 in. (45 cm) scape in midsummer; fertile.

Hosta 'Azure Snow'

Hosta 'Baby Bunting'

Hosta 'Band of Gold'

Comments: Low light to dappled shade. Leaves soon turn green in very bright light and always become dark green by the end of summer. Among the smallest glaucous-leaved hostas with distinctly corrugated leaves. Grow in containers or as an edging plant in a narrow border. Water sparingly until the roots are established. Slow to increase. Pest resistant. Performs better in cooler climates. Zones 3–7.

Similar: *H.* 'Popo', *H.* 'Tet-A-Poo'.

Sports: *H.* 'Cameo' (leaves with a wide yellow margin), *H.* 'Cherish' (leaves yellow with a dark green margin), *H.* 'Pandora's Box'.

Hosta 'Band of Gold'
Large, marginally variegated leaves.

Clump size & habit: 26½ in. wide × 22 in. high (65 × 55 cm). An upright mound with contrasting leaf color.

Description: Leaf blade 10½ × 8 in. (26 × 20 cm), of thick substance, dark green, very widely margined chartreuse, turning yellow and becoming ivory white, feathered towards the center, matt above, turning glossy, glaucous below, prominently veined, seersuckered, edge slightly rippled, lightly cupped, rounded with heart-shaped pinched lobes. Petiole flattish, dark green, outlined in yellow. Flower pure white with a translucent margin on an upright, leafy, green, 24 in. (60 cm) scape from early to midsummer; fertility unknown.

Comments: Site in moderate shade for most dramatic leaf color. The wide, ivory white margin is a striking contrast to the spinach-green leaf centers which the feathering enhances. Moderate growth rate. Reasonably pest resistant.

Similar: *H.* 'Formal Attire', *H.* 'Robert Frost'.

Hosta 'Betsy King'
Medium, green leaves.

Clump size & habit: 24½ in. wide × 16 in. high (61 × 40 cm). An upright mound.

Description: Leaf blade 4¾ × 2½ in. (12 × 6 cm), of average substance, glossy, dark green, closely veined, some dimpling when mature, edge shallowly undulate, flat, oval with a recurved tip and tapered, open to pinched lobes. Petiole dark green. Flower rich purple, in abundance, on an upright, leafy, dark green, 30 in. (75 cm) scape in late summer; fertile.

Comments: Light to moderate shade. Not suitable for container growing.

Similar: *H.* 'Decorata Normalis' (leaves slightly smaller).

Hosta 'Big Daddy'
Large, very blue leaves.

Clump size & habit: 41 in. wide × 26 in. high (102 × 65 cm). A dense mound.

Description: Leaf blade 12 × 11½ in. (30 × 29 cm), very thick, rich glaucous blue, turning green toward late summer, strongly seersuckered and puckered, edge almost flat, distinctly cupped, nearly round with heart-shaped folded to overlapping lobes. Petiole stout, paler blue-green. Flower near-white on an upright, bare, paler blue-green, 28 in. (70 cm) scape in midsummer; fertile.

Comments: Leaf color remains a chalky dark blue in well-shaded sites for most of the summer. Pest resistant. Very slow growing, especially from tissue-cultured plants. Among the most distinctly cupped, larger, blue-leaved hostas.

Similar: *H.* 'Aksarben', *H.* 'Aqua Velva', *H.* 'Bressingham Blue', *H.* 'Lakeside Blue Jeans'.

Sports: *H.* 'Sugar Daddy' (leaves blue with a white margin).

Hosta 'Betsy King'

Hosta 'Big Daddy'

Hosta 'Big John'

Giant, gray-green leaves.

Clump size & habit: 51 in. wide × 28 in. high (127 × 65 cm). A dense mound of overlapping leaves.

Description: Leaf blade 18 × 15 in. (45 × 38 cm), of thick substance, dark bluish green soon becoming dark green, dimpled, edge flat to slightly rippled, arching, widely oval with heart-shaped overlapping lobes. Petiole stout, glaucous light green. Flower bell-shaped, white-striped pale lavender, level with or just above the leaf mound, in dense clusters on an upright, bare, glaucous green, 32 in. (80 cm) scape in mid to late summer; fertile.

Comments: Rapidly exceeds its registered dimensions to become one of the largest hostas both in clump size and individual leaf size. Most of the glaucous bloom on the upper leaf surface is toward the midrib. Underside of the leaf is gray-green, and the general effect of the leaves is gray-green.

Hosta 'Big John'

Hosta 'Big Mama'

Large, blue-green leaves.

Clump size & habit: 60 in. wide × 26 in. high (150 × 65 cm). A mound of overlapping leaves.

Description: Leaf blade 18 × 14 in. (45 × 35 cm), of thick substance, glaucous dark blue-green, seersuckered and puckered, veins deeply ribbed, edge rippled, arching to convex, undulate near the well-defined tip, widely oval with heart-shaped pinched lobes. Petiole stout, pale

Hosta 'Big Mama'

blue-green. Flower bell-shaped, palest lavender, on an upright, bare, gray-green, 42½ in. (106 cm) scape from midsummer; fertile.

Comments: Provide good light to full shade. Tolerates some morning sun in cooler climates, but with more sun the blue leaf color disappears. Very floriferous. A useful background hosta. Slow to establish. Pest resistant.

Hosta 'Bigfoot'

Giant, blue-green leaves.

Clump size & habit: 69 in. wide × 30½ in. high (173 × 76 cm). A tiered mound.

Description: Leaf blade 18¾ × 12 in. (47 × 30 cm), of thick substance, mid blue-green, dimpled, widely spaced and moderately prominent veins, edges slightly rippled, nearly flat, widely oval with heart-shaped overlapping lobes. Petiole gray-green. Flower near-white on an upright, bare, glaucous green, 31 in. (78 cm) scape in midsummer; fertile.

Comments: Shade. Protect from harsh winds. Slow growth rate initially, then moderate growth rate. Pest resistant.

Hosta 'Blazing Saddles'

Large, marginally variegated leaves.

Clump size & habit: 44½ in. wide × 18 in. high (112 × 45 cm). A symmetrical mound with contrasting colors.

Description: Leaf blade 8¾ × 8 in. (22 × 20 cm), of good substance, emerging light green, becoming dark, widely and irregularly margined pale cream to white with gray-green streaking,

Hosta 'Blazing Saddles'

Hosta 'Bigfoot'

glaucous above and matt below, widely veined, seersuckered, edge almost flat, lightly cupped, oblong to oval with flat, pinched lobes. Petiole narrowly channeled, dark green, outlined in white. Flower bell-shaped, lavender on an upright, bare, green, 28½ in. (71 cm) scape from early to midsummer; fertile.

Comments: Light shade but some morning sun in cooler gardens. Slow to moderate growth rate. Pest resistant. A superb border plant accentuated by accompanying contrasting lacy foliage.

Similar: *H.* 'Bobbie Sue' (leaves wider).

Hosta 'Blond Elf'

Hosta 'Blue Angel'

Hosta 'Blond Elf'

Small, yellowish leaves.

Clump size & habit: 24 in. wide × 8½ in. high (60 × 21 cm). A dense, dome-shaped mound.

Description: Leaf blade 4½ × 2 in. (11 × 5 cm), of thin substance, chartreuse to muted yellow-gold, matt above and shiny below, closely veined, edge widely rippled, concave, oval, narrowing to a graceful tip, lobes tapered and open. Petiole narrowly channeled, chartreuse. Flower lavender on an upright, leafy, chartreuse, 14 in. (35 cm) scape in high to late summer; fertile.

Comments: Lutescent. Tolerates morning sun in cooler climates in spite of the thin leaves. Color holds well into autumn. Rapid growth rate. Useful for edging or at the front of the border.

Similar: *H.* 'Devon Gold', **H.* 'Lemon Lime'.

Hosta 'Blue Angel'

Giant, blue-gray leaves.

Clump size & habit: 71 in. wide × 36 in. (178 × 90 cm). A graceful, cascading mound.

Description: Leaf blade 16 × 12 in. (40 × 30 cm), of thick substance, glaucous dark blue-gray to dark blue-green, slight dimpling when mature, prominently and closely ribbed veins, edge rippled, arching, convex, widely oval to wedge-shaped with a distinct tip and with heart-shaped pinched lobes. Petiole gray-green. Flower long lasting, palest lavender to near-white in a dense raceme on a stout, upright, leafy, gray-green, 48 in. (120 cm) scape in midsummer; fertile.

Comments: Grow in a few hours of morning sun in cooler climates followed by light shade in the afternoon. Among the best large, blue-leaved hostas in warm climates. Tolerates very dry soil when fully established.

Sports: *H.* 'Angel Eyes' (leaves viridescent white to light green with a dark blue margin), *H.* 'Duke of Cornwall', **H.* 'Earth Angel', *H.* 'Fallen Angel' (leaves emerge white with green speckling before turning all green), **H.* 'Guardian Angel', *H.* 'Grey Ghost' (leaves emerge translucent white before turning yellow and finally blue).

Hosta 'Blue Arrow'

Medium, blue-green leaves.

Clump size & habit: 24 in. wide × 18 in. high (60 × 45 cm). A semi-upright, arching mound.

Description: Leaf blade 8½ × 3½ in. (21 × 9 cm), of good substance, blue-green, pale glaucous green below, smooth, widely veined, edge widely undulate and slightly upturned, widely lance-shaped narrowing to a point and with heart-shaped, open, broad lobes. Petiole pale green. Flower bell-shaped, near-white, on an upright, bare, 16 in. (40 cm) scape in high summer; very fertile.

Comments: Tolerates some morning sun in cooler climates, but the leaves remain bluer for longer in dappled to light shade. Pest resistant.

Similar: *H.* 'Deane's Dream', *H.* 'Hadspen Heron', *H.* 'Happiness', *H.* 'Kiwi Blue Heron', *H.* 'Pineapple Poll'.

Hosta 'Blue Arrow'

Hosta 'Blue Boy'

Medium, blue-green leaves.

Clump size & habit: 45½ in. wide × 15 in. high (114 × 38 cm). A dense mound.

Description: Leaf blade 8½ × 5 in. (21 × 13 cm), of average substance, soft blue soon turning green, smooth, prominently veined, edge slightly rippled, folded, widely oval with heart-shaped pinched to overlapping lobes. Petiole thin, light blue-green. Flower pale lavender to near-white in profusion on an upright, leafy, light green, 22 in. (55 cm) scape in midsummer; fertile.

Comments: Dappled shade. Vigorous, fast growing. Use as a ground cover or edging plant.

Similar: *H.* 'Fond Hope', *H.* 'Goldbrook Genie'.

Sports: *H.* 'Bolt Out of the Blue' (leaf margin gold to cream), *H.* 'Deja Blu'.

Hosta 'Blue Boy'

Hosta 'Blue Cadet'

Medium, blue-green leaves.

Clump size & habit: 30 in. wide × 15 in. high (75 × 38 cm). A symmetrical, dense mound.

Description: Leaf blade 5 × 4 in. (13 × 10 cm), of average substance, blue-green, slight

Hosta 'Blue Cadet'

dimpling when mature, edge flat, widely oval with cupped and folded lobes. Petiole narrowly channeled, light gray-green. Flower rich lavender in a long, dense raceme on an upright, bare, light green, 22 in. (55 cm) scape from mid to late summer; fertile.

Comments: Provide light shade all day, but even so leaves will turn dark green by late summer. Magnificent flowers. Vigorous, fast growing.

Similar: *H.* 'Banyai's Dancing Girl', **H.* 'Blue Boy', *H.* 'Drummer Boy', *H.* 'Goldbrook Genie', *H.* 'My Blue Heaven', *H.* 'Pacific Blue Edger', *H.* 'Saint Fiacre', *H.* 'Serendipity'.

Sports: *H.* 'Medal of Honor' (leaf margin cream), *H.* 'Toy Soldier' (leaf margin bicolored).

Hosta 'Blue Flame'

Medium, marginally variegated leaves.

Clump size & habit: 36 in. wide × 15 in. high (90 × 38 cm). A dome-shaped mound.

Description: Leaf blade 8½ × 6½ in. (21 × 16 cm), of thick substance, smooth powdery pale blue, irregularly margined cream turning yellow, with gray-green streaking and white flashes along the outer rim of the margin, dimpled, edge almost flat, convex, widely oval with heart-shaped lobes. Petiole blue-green, outlined in cream. Flower slightly fragrant, white, opening from a rich violet bud, on an upright, bare, blue-green scape up to 30 in. (75 cm), with unusually large, leafy bracts toward the top of the scape, in high summer; fertile.

Comments: Site in good light to dappled shade to maintain the powdery bloom on the leaf surface. Vigorous. Pest resistant. The attractive tricolored margin is visible on mature plants. The marginal variegation appears after the leaves have expanded. The fragrance is only perceptible in warm climates.

Similar: *H.* 'Frosted Dimples' (leaf surface more seersuckered), *H.* 'Secret Love' (leaf margin wider).

Hosta 'Blue Flame'

Hosta 'Blue Hawaii'

Large to giant, very blue leaves.

Clump size & habit: 42¾ in. wide × 30½ in. high (107 × 76 cm). An upright mound of outward-facing leaves.

Description: Leaf blade 10 × 8 in. (25 × 20 cm), of thick substance, heavily glaucous rich powdery blue, prominently veined, seersuckered, edge flat, oval to heart-shaped, open to pinched lobes. Petiole blue-green. Flower bell-shaped, lightly fragrant, white in a prolific display on an upright, leafy, pale blue-green, 43½ in. (109 cm) scape from mid to late summer; fertile.

Comments: Needs light shade to retain good leaf color which can hold till summer's end. Vigorous. Pest resistant. A superb specimen or border plant.

Hosta 'Blue Hawaii'

Hosta 'Blue Jay'

Small, very blue leaves.

Clump size & habit: 25 in. wide × 10 in. high (63 × 25 cm). A compact mound.

Description: Leaf blade 6 × 4 in. (15 × 10 cm), of thick substance, intense dark blue turning dark green, dimpled, edge almost flat, folded to cupped, widely oval to nearly round with a vestigial tip and heart-shaped pinched to overlapping lobes. Petiole narrowly channeled, blue-green. Flower bell-shaped, white, on an upright, bare, pale blue-green, 12 in. (30 cm) scape in high summer; exceptionally fertile.

Comments: Dappled to medium shade. Slow growing. Pest resistant. Zones 3–9.

Similar: *H.* 'Dorset Blue'.

Hosta 'Blue Jay'

Hosta 'Blue Moon'

Hosta 'Blue Mouse Ears'

Hosta 'Blue Moon'
Small, dark blue leaves.

Clump size & habit: 12 in. wide × 8½ in. high (30 × 21 cm). A neat, flattish mound.

Description: Leaf blade 4½ × 4½ in. (11 × 11 cm), very thick, rich dark blue, some dimpling when mature, edge slightly undulate, cupped, widely oval to nearly round with a small tip and heart-shaped open to folded lobes. Petiole short, near horizontal, blue-gray. Flower near-white to lavender-gray in a dense raceme on an upright, bare, blue-gray, 8¾ in. (22 cm) scape in mid to high summer; fertile.

Comments: Dappled to medium shade. Slow growing. Pest resistant. Zones 3–9.

Similar: *H.* 'Blue Ice', **H.* 'Kiwi Blue Baby'.

Hosta 'Blue Mouse Ears'
Small, blue-green leaves.

Clump size & habit: 11 in. wide × 6½ in. high (28 × 16 cm). An open mound of horizontal leaves.

Description: Leaf blade 2½ × 2 in. (6 × 5 cm), very thick, almost rubbery, rich blue-green, some dimpling, edge almost flat, shallowly cupped, oval when young, nearly round with a vestigial tip and heart-shaped open lobes. Petiole stout, shallowly channeled, dark green. Flower superb clusters of bell-shaped, rich violet-striped lavender, on a

thick, upright, leafy, pale green, 8½ in. (21 cm) scape in mid to high summer; sterile.

Comments: Grow in some morning sun in cooler climates, elsewhere in good light to light shade. Moderate growth rate. Reasonably pest resistant. Flowers are striking especially when in bud. Buds are held horizontally and swell up like mini-balloons before partially opening. An excellent specimen for a rock garden, gravel bed, or container.

Similar: **H.* 'Baby Bunting', **H.* 'Popo'.

Hosta 'Blue River'
Medium, marginally variegated leaves.

Clump size & habit: 30½ in. wide × 15 in. high (76 × 38 cm). An arching mound.

Description: Leaf blade 8¾ × 7½ in. (22 × 19 cm), of thick substance, rich dark blue, widely and irregularly margined chartreuse turning yellow, shiny above and a thick glaucous blue-gray below, seersuckered, edge slightly undulate, convex, broadly oval with heart-shaped pinched to folded lobes. Petiole stout, glaucous blue-green. Flower near-white in a dense raceme on a leaning, bare, blue-green, 18 in. (45 cm) scape in midsummer; fertile.

Comments: Site in moderate shade to retain the subtle contrasts between the leaf margin, leaf center, and intermediate chartreuse streak-

Hosta 'Blue River'

ing. Not suitable for containers. Slow to moderate growth rate. Pest resistant. Differs from its parent *H.* 'True Blue' in having a considerably smaller habit and a shiny upper leaf surface. Zones 3–7.

Similar: *H.* 'Bingo' and *H.* 'Brave Amherst' (leaf margin narrower), *H.* 'Fleeta Brownell Woodroffe', *H.* 'Tokudama Aureomarginata'.

Hosta 'Blue Sliver'

Small, blue-gray.

Clump size & habit: 15 in. wide × 6 in. high (38 × 15 cm). An unruly mound.

Description: Leaf blade 4½ × up to 2 in. (11 × 5 cm), of good substance, glaucous rich blue-gray, smooth, flat when mature, lanceolate to wedge-shaped with a strongly acute tip, decurrent with the narrow, glaucous blue-gray petiole. Flower lavender on an upright, bare, 12 in. (30 cm) scape in late summer; fertility unknown.

Comments: Light shade. An ideal specimen for a small container or at the front of a border with ferns and foliage of a contrasting leaf color. Slow growing. Zones 3–7.

Hosta 'Bob Olson'

Small, marginally variegated leaves.

Clump size & habit: 12 in. wide × 5 in. high (30 × 13 cm). A dense mound.

Description: Leaf blade 3 × 2 in. (8 × 5 cm), of good substance, satiny, dark olive green, irregularly margined creamy white, moderately prominent veining, edge slightly rippled, slightly undulate, somewhat folded, lanceolate to elliptic with an acute tip and rounded, open to pinched lobes. Petiole dark green, outlined in ivory. Flower bell-shaped on an upright, leafy, purple-flecked green, 16 in. (40 cm) scape in late summer; fertility unknown.

Comments: Performs well in sun for a half day except in the hottest regions. Fast growing.

Hosta 'Bold Ruffles'

Giant, blue-gray leaves.

Clump size & habit: 36 in. wide × 30 in. high (90 × 75 cm). A stiff, upright, somewhat unruly mound.

Description: Leaf blade 15 × 12 in. (38 × 30 cm), very thick, blue-gray, seersuckered and crumpled, edge distinctly rippled especially on juvenile leaves, oval to nearly round with a twisted tip and heart-shaped pinched to overlapping lobes. Petiole coarse, light gray-green. Flower bell-shaped, near-white, on an upright, leafy, glaucous-gray, 32 in. (80 cm) scape in midsummer; fertile.

Comments: Loses its color during the second half of the season but will retain its blueness longer if grown out of direct sunlight. Avoid planting under trees where the leaves will collect falling debris. Very slow to increase but eventually forms a huge clump. Feed well and water

Hosta 'Blue Sliver'

Hosta 'Bob Olson'

copiously. Pest resistant. Not suitable for containers. Zones 3–9.

Hosta 'Brenda's Beauty'

Medium, medio-variegated leaves.

Clump size & habit: 41 in. wide × 18 in. high (102 × 45 cm). An open mound.

Description: Leaf blade 8 × 5 in. (20 × 13 cm), of moderate substance, emerges pale chartreuse turning yellow and finally ivory, irregularly margined mid to dark green with streaks jetting toward the midrib, matt above and glaucous below, dimpled, strongly marked veins, edge undulate, slightly cupped, widely oval with heart-shaped pinched lobes. Petiole chartreuse to ivory, outlined in dark green. Flower pinkish lavender, opening from a rich violet bud, in a dense raceme on an upright, leafy, glaucous green, 28 in. (70 cm) scape, purple-tinted toward the raceme, in high summer; poor fertility.

Comments: Grow in good light to moderate shade in cooler climates for best leaf color, elsewhere in shade all day. Vigorous. Among the best sports of *H.* 'Gold Standard'; the variegated portion of the leaf has conspicuous netted veining. Divide frequently.

Similar: *H.* 'Something Different'.

Hosta 'Bridegroom'

Small to medium, green leaves.

Clump size & habit: 34 in. wide × 16 in. high (85 × 40 cm). A low mound with upright leaves.

Description: Leaf blade 5 × 4 in. (13 × 10 cm), of thin substance, smooth, glossy, dark olive green, veins prominently marked, edge rippled, triangular, the side of the leaf sloping downward, the center and the twisted tip curving upward, lobes heart-shaped and open. Petiole narrowly channeled, dark green, purple dotted toward the crown. Flower lavender on an upright, bare, green, 18 in. (45 cm) scape in late summer; sterile.

Comments: Light to moderate shade. Slow to moderate growth rate. Leaves uniquely curved upward, hence the name. Vulnerable to pests but worth the extra effort to preserve the leaves intact since this is one of the best of the newer green-leaved hostas. Winner of the 2004 Alex

Hosta 'Bold Ruffles', a young plant.

Hosta 'Brenda's Beauty'

Hosta 'Bridegroom'

J. Summers Distinguished Merit Hosta Award. Zones 3–9.

   Similar: *H.* 'Stirfry'.

Hosta 'Brother Ronald'

Medium, very blue leaves.

   Clump size & habit: 20 in. wide × 15 in. high (50 × 38 cm). A dense mound.

   Description: Leaf blade 6½ × 4 in. (16 × 10 cm), of thick substance, intense mid to dark blue, veins slightly ribbed, dimpled, edge slightly undulate, cupped, widely oval with heart-shaped overlapping lobes. Petiole pale blue-green. Flower bell-shaped, white in dense clusters on an upright, bare, glaucous gray-green, 18¾ in. (47 cm) scape in late summer; fertile.

   Comments: Light to full shade. One of the bluest-leaved hostas but not the most shapely in leaf or clump. Moderate growth rate.

Hosta 'Brother Stephan'

Large, medio-variegated leaves.

   Clump size & habit: 35 in. wide × 22 in. high (88 × 55 cm). An open mound.

   Description: Leaf blade 10¾ × 10 in. (27 × 25 cm), of thick substance, golden yellow, very widely and irregularly margined medium green with chartreuse streaks jetting towards the midrib, matt above and glaucous below, seersuckered, edge flat, lightly cupped, nearly round with heart-shaped pinched to folded lobes. Petiole stout, green, outlined in yellow. Flower bell-shaped, pure white in a dense raceme on an upright, leafy, gray-green, 26½ in. (66 cm) scape in early summer; fertile.

   Comments: Site in light shade in a foliage border where it will stand out among plain green leaves. The variegation exhibits a "hand print" or "maple leaf" design, and the leaf surface has ex-

Hosta 'Brother Ronald'

ceptionally heavy seersuckering. Not suitable for containers. Moderate growth rate. Pest resistant. Divide frequently. Zones 3–7.

Similar: *H.* 'Inniswood', *H.* 'Paradigm', *H.* 'September Sun'.

Hosta 'Buckshaw Blue'

Medium, very blue leaves.

Clump size & habit: 35½ in. wide × 14 in. high (89 × 35 cm). A mound of outward-facing leaves.

Description: Leaf blade 5 × 4½ in. (13 × 11 cm), thick, dark blue above and pale glaucous green below, heavily seersuckered, veins deeply impressed, edge almost flat, markedly cupped toward the lobes, nearly round with a vestigial tip and heart-shaped folded or overlapping lobes. Petiole coarse, shallowly channeled, pale green. Flower bell-shaped, near-white, on an upright, bare, pale green, 18 in. (45 cm) scape in midsummer; fertile.

Comments: The standard by which all blue-leaved hostas should be judged. Heavy, waxy coating on the leaves is retained until late summer in cooler climates, where it produces its best color if grown in full shade. Clear light gives the leaves a much lighter blue appearance. Avoid planting under trees where falling debris can damage the bloom on the leaves. Very slow to increase. Pest resistant.

Similar: *H.* 'Blue Velvet', *H.* 'Moscow Blue', *H.* 'Tokudama'.

Hosta 'Camelot'

Medium, very blue leaves.

Clump size & habit: 34¾ in. wide × 16 in. high (87 × 40 cm). A widely spaced, layered mound.

Description: Leaf blade 7 × 5 in. (18 × 13 cm), of thick substance, intense light blue, seersuckered and puckered, edge flat to slightly undulate, shallowly cupped or convex, heart-shaped to nearly round with a distinct tip and heart-shaped overlapping lobes. Petiole long, light blue-green. Flower bell-shaped, palest lavender, on an upright, bare, blue-green, 18 in. (45 cm) scape in late summer; fertile.

Hosta 'Brother Stephan'

Hosta 'Buckshaw Blue'

Hosta 'Camelot'

Comments: Dappled to light shade. One of the best of the medium-sized pale blue-leaved hostas. Slow to moderate growth rate. Pest resistant.

Similar: **H.* 'Brother Ronald', *H.* 'Sherborne Songbird'.

Hosta 'Candy Cane'

Small, marginally variegated leaves.

Clump size & habit: 14 in. wide × 7 in. high (35 × 18 cm). A diffuse, cascading mound.

Description: Leaf blade 6½ × 2½ in. (16 × 6 cm), of average substance, satiny, dark green, irregularly and variably margined golden yellow fading to cream, some dimpling on mature outer

Hosta 'Candy Cane', in deep shade

Hosta 'Captain Kirk'

leaves, edges rippled, arching, lanceolate to oval with an acute tip and tapered, open lobes. Petiole flattish, dark green. Flower dark purple-striped lavender on an upright, 12¾–16 in. (32–40 cm) scape in late summer; fertility unknown.

Comments: Site in light to moderate shade as the margin will turn white if exposed to direct sunlight. Vigorous, fast growing. Suitable for edging in light woodland. Not suitable for containers.

Similar: **H.* 'Resonance'.

Hosta 'Captain Kirk'

Medium, medio-variegated leaves.

Clump size & habit: 36 in. wide × 20 in. high (90 × 50 cm). A mound of overlapping leaves.

Description: Leaf blade 9 × 7 in. (23 × 18 cm), of good substance, emerging chartreuse turning first yellow then ivory, widely margined bright midgreen, matt above and glaucous below, dimpled, strongly veined, edge almost flat, slightly arching, slightly convex, widely oval with a vestigial tip and heart-shaped pinched lobes. Petiole flattish, cream-colored, finely outlined in dark green. Flower pinkish lavender, opening from a rich violet bud, in a dense raceme on an upright, leafy, glaucous green, 28 in. (70 cm) scape, purple-tinted toward the raceme, in high summer; poor fertility.

Comments: Benefits from some morning sun. Careful positioning needed for best color effect. The margin can be up to 2¾ in. (7 cm) wide. Differs from its parent *H.* 'Gold Standard' in having thicker leaves with a narrower central variegation, and in holding its color better. Divide frequently. Vigorous, fairly fast growing.

Similar: **H.* 'Ann Kulpa'.

Hosta 'Carnival'

Medium to large, marginally variegated leaves.

Clump size & habit: 41 in. wide × 16–18 in. high (102 × 40–45 cm). An open mound.

Description: Leaf blade 9 × 7½ in. (23 × 19 cm), of thick substance, mid to dark green-blue to green-gray, widely and irregularly margined yellow to cream with gray-green streaking and mottling, matt above and glaucous below, mature leaves intensely seersuckered, edge slightly rippled, convex, oval to heart-shaped with a vestigial tip and heart-shaped open lobes. Petiole widely channeled, green, strongly outlined in cream. Flower long-lasting, lavender, opening from a purple bud, on a stout, upright, leafy, glaucous gray-green, 30 in. (75 cm) scape in midsummer; fertile.

Comments: Provide light to full shade. Leaves lose their intense color in too much sun. Wide margins are distinctly feathered with two-tone mottling. Flower scapes are held well above the leaf mound with attractive large variegated bracts. Slow to establish but eventually a strikingly colorful mound.

Similar: *H.* 'Carousel' (habit smaller, leaves not as shapely), *H.* 'Cavalcade' (leaves lack mottling and streaking).

Hosta 'Carnival', in deep shade

Hosta 'Carolina Sunshine'

Medium, marginally variegated leaves.

Clump size & habit: 41 in. wide × 14 in. high (102 × 35 cm). A dense, unruly mound.

Description: Leaf blade 9 × 5 in. (23 × 13 cm), of thinnish substance, glossy, mid to dark green, widely and very irregularly margined and splashed butterscotch yellow turning cream, widely veined, edge conspicuously rippled, arching, elliptic with an acute tip and tapered, pinched lobes. Petiole narrowly channeled, dark green, finely outlined in cream. Flower lavender on an upright, leafy, green, 20 in. (50 cm) scape in late summer; fertile.

Comments: Sun tolerant even in warmer climates. Fast and easy.

Similar: *H.* 'Yellow Splash Rim' (not sun tolerant).

Hosta 'Carolina Sunshine', a young plant.

Hosta 'Cascades'

Medium, medio-variegated leaves.

Clump size & habit: 26 in. wide × 15 in. high (65 × 38 cm). A spectacular, open, arching mound.

Description: Leaf blade 11 × 4½ in. (28 × 11 cm), of thinnish substance, smooth, matt, ivory white, widely margined dark green with some chartreuse streaks jetting toward the midrib, edge

Hosta 'Cascades'

undulate, arching toward the sometimes curved, acute tip, oval with rounded, open to pinched lobes. Petiole ivory, outlined in dark green. Flower white on a leaning, leafy, ivory white, 36 in. (90 cm) scape in early summer; fertile.

Comments: Not always easy, needing summer heat and regular feeding to attain optimum size. For best results, provide two hours of morning sun followed by light shade. Site in the center of a border of plain green- or blue-leaved hostas for maximum effect. Divide frequently.

Hosta 'Cathedral Windows', a young plant.

Hosta 'Cat's Eye'

Hosta 'Cathedral Windows'

Medium to large, medio-variegated leaves.

Clump size & habit: 34½ in. wide × 19 in. high (86 × 48 cm). A dome-shaped, open mound.

Description: Leaf blade 10 × 9 in. (25 × 23 cm), of good substance, matt golden yellow with a very wide, irregular dark green margin with some chartreuse streaking, dimpled, strongly and widely veined, edge slightly undulate, convex, broadly oval to rounded with a pointed tip and flat to heart-shaped, open to pinched lobes. Petiole chartreuse, outlined in dark green. Flower large, very fragrant, near-white, radially arranged, on an upright, pale green, 36 in. (90 cm) scape, with occasional large variegated bracts toward the raceme, in late summer; usually sterile.

Comments: Full sun all day, except in the hottest climates, and abundant moisture are needed to produce a prolific display of flowers. Differs from its parent *H.* 'Stained Glass' in having much wider leaf margins which entirely change the balance of the leaf color. Rapid growth rate. Divide frequently. Zones 3–9.

Similar: *H.* 'Avocado' and **H.* 'Holy Molé' (leaf margin somewhat wider).

Hosta 'Cat's Eye'

Miniature, medio-variegated leaves.

Clump size & habit: 6 in. wide × 2 in. high (15 × 5 cm). A low, dense mound.

Description: Leaf blade 1½ × ½ in. (4 × 1 cm), of thin substance, smooth, matt yellow turning ivory, irregularly margined dark olive green with streaks jetting toward the midrib, edge flat with occasional kinks, folded, lanceolate with an acute tip and tapered, open lobes. Petiole narrowly channeled, ivory white, outlined in dark green. Flower attractive, rich purple with a near-white throat on a leaning, bare, ridged, 14 in. (35 cm) scape in late summer; fertile.

Comments: Albescent. Not easy to grow. Good light to light shade with some morning sun in cooler climates. Until roots are well established, keep it in a pot and do not divide. A free-draining soil will boost turgidity and vigor, but the growth rate will always be slow. Best suited to a trough, sink, or rock garden with other miniature hostas and tiny ferns. A two-tone effect in the central variegation at midsummer between the first flush of leaves that then assume a yellow variegation and the newly emerging leaves with ivory white centers.

Similar: *H.* 'Cherish' (leaves rounder, more robust), **H.* 'Cracker Crumbs'.

Hosta 'Chartreuse Wiggles'

Small, yellowish leaves.

Clump size & habit: 25 in. wide × 10 in. high (63 × 25 cm). A dense, spreading mound.

Description: Leaf blade 5 × 1 in. (13 × 2.5 cm), of thin substance, satiny, smooth, bright chartreuse to golden yellow, veins closely ribbed, edge distinctly rippled, arching, elliptic with an acute tip and tapered, open lobes. Petiole flattish, chartreuse. Flower bell-shaped, purple-striped lavender on a thin, upright, bare, pale chartreuse, 18 in. (45 cm) scape in late summer; fertile.

Comments: Lutescent. Best in a hot climate with high humidity and sufficient moisture at the roots to boost its singular lack of vigor. Can be successful in cooler climates, when grown in a container, despite its rhizomatous habit. Protect from bright sunlight and strong winds. Creates a restless, sinuous effect when planted as a foreground specimen or edger accompanying larger hostas, either echoing almost linear leaves or contrasting round or heart-shaped leaves.

Similar: *H.* 'Chartreuse Waves' (leaves wider), **H.* 'Dragon Tails', *H.* 'Sea Wiggles', *H. sieboldii* 'Subcrocea', *H.* 'Yellow Submarine' (somewhat larger and easier to cultivate).

Hosta 'Cheatin Heart'

Small, yellowish leaves.

Clump size & habit: 18 in. wide × 8½ in. high (45 × 21 cm). A compact mound.

Description: Leaf blade 2½ × 1¼ in. (6 × 3 cm), of thin substance, matt chartreuse turning rich golden yellow, slightly dimpled, veins green, edge rippled, folded, oval, heart-shaped to flat pinched lobes. Petiole narrowly channeled, pale green. Flower lavender on an upright, bare, yellow, 7½–10 in. (19–25 cm) scape from mid to high summer; fertile.

Comments: Lutescent. Leaf color can intensify to orange-gold in sunlight. Moderate growth rate. Ideal for a rock garden with dwarf variegated London pride (*Saxifraga ×urbium*) at its feet.

Similar: *H.* 'Heartbroken' (a sport of *H.* 'Faithful Heart' with viridescent golden yellow leaves).

Hosta 'Chartreuse Wiggles'

Hosta 'Cheatin Heart'

Hosta 'Cherry Berry'

Sports: *H.* 'Faithful Heart' and *H.* 'Stolen Kiss' (leaves yellow with a green margin), *H.* 'Illicit Affair' (leaves green with a yellow margin).

Hosta 'Cherry Berry'

Small to medium, medio-variegated leaves.

Clump size & habit: 14 in. wide × 10 in. high (35 × 25 cm). A diffuse, upright mound.

Description: Leaf blade 6½ × 2½ in. (16 × 6 cm), of thin substance, smooth, satiny, emerging yellow turning ivory, irregularly and widely margined dark olive green with some chartreuse streaks jetting toward the midrib, edge with occasional shallow undulations, arching toward the tip, elliptic with an acute, sometimes curved or pinched, tip and with tapered, open lobes. Petiole flattish, pink-tinted ivory, widely outlined in dark olive green. Flower violet, subtended by cream bracts, on an upright, leafy, glossy, intense burgundy red, 28 in. (70 cm) scape in high summer; seedpods red; fertility unknown.

Comments: Benefits from morning sun or very good light. Leaves widen considerably in hot climates where growth is more vigorous. A tricolor effect is often visible on the leaves in early to midsummer making it worthwhile to give this hosta special care. The burgundy red scapes and red seedpods are other reasons to persevere. Susceptible to pest damage. Divide frequently.

Similar: *H.* 'Celebration', *H.* 'Hot Lips'; *H.* 'Joyce Trott'.

Sports: *H.* 'Maraschino Cherry' (leaves dark green).

Hosta 'Chinese Sunrise'

Small to medium, medio-variegated leaves.

Clump size & habit: 28 in. wide × 14 in. high (70 × 35 cm). A dense, arching mound.

Description: Leaf blade 6½ × 3 in. (16 × 8 cm), of thin substance, smooth, chartreuse-yellow fading to light olive green, narrowly and irregularly margined dark olive green, glossy above and satiny below, prominently veined, edge slightly undulate, lanceolate with an acute tip and tapered, open lobes. Petiole narrowly channeled, olive green. Flower bell-shaped, light purple, in

Hosta 'Chinese Sunrise'

clusters on a thin, somewhat leaning, very leafy, 28 in. (70 cm) scape in late summer; fertile.

Comments: Viridescent. One of the first to emerge in spring. Site in morning sun to good light to retain the variegation for as long as possible. Because the leaves gradually change color through the season, it is best to plant this hosta in clumps 12 in. (30 cm) apart as an edger or in masses as a groundcover. Good in containers.

Hosta 'Christmas Candy'

Medium, medio-variegated leaves.

Clump size & habit: 24 in. wide × 18 in. high (60 × 45 cm). An upright clump.

Description: Leaf blade 7½ × 3 in. (19 × 8 cm), of thick substance, emerging chartreuse, turning ivory, widely and irregularly margined dark green, randomly streaked towards the midrib, satiny above and shiny below, widely veined, edge slightly rippled, undulate to twisting, oval with a graceful tip and heart-shaped open to pinched lobes. Petiole flattish, ivory, finely outlined in dark green. Flower drooping, pale lav-

Hosta 'Christmas Candy'

ender, on an upright, leafy, ivory, 25 in. (63 cm) scape in midsummer; sterile.

Comments: Morning sun followed by light shade. Can take more sun in cooler climates provided adequate moisture is available. A weak chartreuse overlay is apparent in the whitish variegation towards the petiole; the leaf center

Hosta
'Christmas Tree'

Hosta
'Cinnamon Sticks'

remains pristine ivory throughout the season. The flower heads die less than gracefully so remove them as they start to wither. Lovely with asarums and tradescantia. Divide frequently.

Similar: *H.* 'Christmas Cookies', *H.* 'Undulata', and *H.* 'White Christmas' (leaves of thinner substance).

Hosta 'Christmas Tree'

Medium to large, marginally variegated leaves.

Clump size & habit: 36 in. wide × 20 in. high (90 × 50 cm). A somewhat unruly mound.

Description: Leaf blade 8½ × 6½ in. (21 × 16 cm), very thick, olive green to dark green with a slight blue cast early in the summer, narrowly and irregularly margined cream turning white, some transitional gray-green streaking jetting toward the midrib, matt above and glaucous below, intensely seersuckered, edge slightly rippled, widely oval to nearly round with a tiny tip and heart-shaped pinched lobes. Petiole dark green, finely outlined in white. Flower pale lavender on an upright, leafy, glaucous green, 18 in. (45 cm) scape in mid to late summer; seedpods red; fertile.

Hosta 'Climax'

Comments: Tolerates two hours of morning sun in cooler climates. Good as a specimen or in a large container. Pest resistant. In full bloom, the outline is pyramidal, having a fancied resemblance to a Christmas tree.

Similar: *H.* 'Grand Master', *H.* 'Van Wade'.

Sports: *H.* 'Christmas Gold', *H.* 'Christmas Pageant' (leaf margin wider).

Hosta 'Cinnamon Sticks'

Small to medium, green leaves.

Clump size & habit: 24 in. wide × 10 in. high (60 × 25 cm). A low, open mound.

Description: Leaf blade 6 × 4½ in. (15 × 11 cm), of thick substance, leathery, light green, matt above and thickly glaucous below, widely veined, edge flat but kinked toward the overlapping, heart-shaped to nearly round lobes. Petiole widely and shallowly channeled, dotted claret-purple back and front and continuing into the palm of the leaf blade. Flower bell-shaped, lavender, in dense clusters on a leaning, leafy, claret-purple dotted, 14 in. (35 cm) scape in late summer and early autumn; fertile.

Comments: Provide light to moderate shade. Lovely with *Heuchera* 'Cathedral Windows', whose pewter and burgundy marbling echoes the burgundy petioles of this hosta.

Similar: *H.* 'Chopsticks' (leaves rounder with a thickly coated white back), **H.* 'One Man's Treasure'.

Hosta 'Climax'

Large, marginally variegated leaves.

Clump size & habit: 51 in. wide × 24½ in. high (127 × 61 cm). A striking vase-shaped mound.

Description: Leaf blade 12 × 10 in. (30 × 25 cm), of average substance, rich mid to dark green, very widely and irregularly margined and feathered bright golden yellow, matt above and slightly glaucous below, heavily seersuckered, edge shallowly undulate, cupped at the base, then arching, nearly round with folded lobes. Petiole midgreen, outlined in yellow. Flower near-white to palest lavender on an upright, glaucous green, 36 in. (90 cm) scape from mid to late summer; seedpods very long; fertile.

Comments: Light shade. Tolerates morning sun in cooler gardens. Pest resistant. Best used in a border with other hostas or foliage plants of a plainer habit. Zones 3–9.

Similar: **H.* 'Afternoon Delight'.

Hosta 'Corkscrew'

Small, green leaves.

Clump size & habit: 22 in. wide × up to 9 in. high (55 × 23 cm). A strikingly unsymmetrical, upright to arching mound.

Description: Leaf blade 7 × 2 in. (18 × 5 cm), of thick substance, mid to dark green, glossy above, very shiny below, veins closely ribbed, edge flat, arching, lanceolate, contorted with

Hosta 'Corkscrew'

Hosta 'Cornbelt', a young plant.

a recurved exaggerated tip, burgundy-purple towards the base, decurrent with the narrowly channeled, short, green petiole. Flower lavender on an upright to slightly leaning, sometimes arched, leafy, brownish green, 18 in. (45 cm) thin scape in early autumn; fertile.

Comments: Light to moderate shade. The contorted leaves give a restless countenance. Best in a container in a border with ferns or plants of unusual leaf shapes. Rapid growth rate. Pest resistant. A worthy winner of the Best Seedling award at the 2002 American Hosta Society's First Look event. Winner of the 2003 Alex J. Summers Distinguished Merit Hosta Award. Zones 3–9.

Similar: *H.* 'Praying Hands' (habit larger and more upright), *H.* 'Tortifrons' (habit smaller, leaves narrower).

Hosta 'Cornbelt'

Medium, medio-variegated leaves.

Clump size & habit: 48 in. wide × 20 in. high (120 × 50 cm). An open, upright mound.

Description: Leaf blade 8½ × 5 in. (21 × 13 cm), of good substance, chartreuse to bright golden yellow, very widely and irregularly margined mid to dark green with chartreuse and dark green streaking, satiny above and thinly glaucous below, heavily furrowed veining, dimpled when mature, edge heavily rippled, slightly folded and arching, oval with a pointed tip, heart-shaped pinched lobes. Petiole chartreuse, outlined in dark green. Flower near-white in dense clusters on an upright, leafy, chartreuse, 24–30 in. (60–75 cm) scape in early summer; fertile.

Comments: Good light or dappled shade in the morning followed by full shade. On mature leaves the deeply seersuckered areas resemble blistering. Moderate growth rate. Pest resistant. A dramatic specimen hosta better suited to a sophisticated shade border than a woodland setting. The prominently piecrusted edges and extravagantly wide dark green margin make it one of the best medium-sized hostas. Divide frequently.

Hosta 'Country Mouse'

Miniature, marginally variegated leaves.

Clump size & habit: 9 in. wide × 2½ in. high (23 × 6 cm). A dense irregular mound.

Description: Leaf blade 2½ × 1½ in. (6 × 4 cm), of good substance, glaucous blue-green narrowly and irregularly margined white, widely veined, dimpled, edge randomly kinked, shallowly cupped, broadly oval with flat, open lobes. Petiole shallowly channeled, blue-green to gray-green, outlined in white. Flower bell-shaped, lavender-striped blushed lavender on a leaning to upright, leafy, dark green scape up to 18 in. (45 cm) in high summer; fertility unknown.

Comments: Moderate light to light shade. Best suited to cooler gardens since the leaves assume a gray-green cast in hotter regions. The much darker blue-green scape towers above the leaf mound. Suitable for sinks, troughs, and pebble gardens. Not as vigorous growing as its parent, *H.* 'Bill Dress's Blue'.

Hosta 'Country Mouse'

Hosta 'Cracker Crumbs'

Hosta 'Crepe Suzette'

Hosta **'Cracker Crumbs'**

Miniature, medio-variegated leaves.

Clump size & habit: 12 in. wide × 6½ in. high (30 × 16 cm). A low mound.

Description: Leaf blade 3 × 2 in. (8 × 5 cm), of good substance, smooth, glossy, copper-tinted golden yellow, irregularly margined emerald green with streaking, prominently veined, edge widely rippled, oval with an acute tip and heart-shaped pinched lobes. Petiole chartreuse. Flower lavender on an upright, chartreuse, leafy, 18 in. (45 cm) scape in late summer; fertile.

Comments: Grow in morning sun and give plenty of water. Vigorous, fast growing. Ideal for sinks, troughs, or gravel gardens. The contrasting emerald green margin appears to have been painted onto the leaf. Divide frequently.

Similar: **H.* 'Cat's Eye'.

Hosta **'Crepe Suzette'**

Small, marginally variegated leaves.

Clump size & habit: 15 in. wide × 7 in. high (38 × 18 cm). An open mound.

Description: Leaf blade 5 × 2 in. (13 × 5 cm), of moderate substance, dark green, widely margined crisp white turning cream, matt above and satiny below, strongly veined, edge slightly undulate, oval with a rounded tip and tapered, open lobes. Petiole flat, widely channeled, dark green, outlined in white. Flower lavender on a leaning, leafy, dark green, 10–12 in. (25–30 cm) scape in late summer; fertile.

Comments: Light to moderate shade. Slow growth rate.

Similar: *H.* 'Cream Cheese' (smaller), *H.* 'Decorata' (habit rhizomatous, leaves larger), *H.* 'Moon River' (leaves rounder, more cupped).

Hosta **'Crispula'**

Large, marginally variegated leaves.

Clump size & habit: 36 in. wide × 20 in. high (90 × 50 cm). A dense, rippling mound.

Hosta 'Crispula'

Hosta 'Cutting Edge'

Description: Leaf blade 12 × 6 in. (30 × 15 cm), of good substance, dark olive green, irregularly margined pure white with gray-green streaking, satiny above and shiny below, deeply depressed veins, some dimpling, edge dramatically rippled, arching, oval with a distinctly twisted tip and heart-shaped pinched lobes. Petiole narrowly channeled, dark green, finely outlined in white. Flower palest lavender on a pendant, leafy, green, 24–36 in. (60–90 cm) scape in early summer; seedpods numerous; fertile.

Comments: Good light to moderate shade. Slow to establish. Prone to virus infection. The leaves twist through 180° making it distinct.

Decorative, flowerlike bracts extend the length of the scape.

Similar: *H.* 'Enchantment', *H. montana* 'Mountain Snow', *H.* 'Snow Crust', *H.* 'Spring Fling' (larger), *H.* 'Zippity Do Dah'.

Sports: *H.* 'Minuet' (smaller).

Hosta 'Cutting Edge'

Medium to large, gray-green leaves.

Clump size & habit: 27 in. wide × 22 in. high (68 × 55 cm). A dense, tiered mound.

Description: Leaf blade 11½ × 6½ in. (29 × 16 cm), of good substance, gray-green with a blue cast, satiny above and distinctly glaucous below, closely spaced veins, dimpled when mature, edge heavily rippled, folded, slightly arching, oval with an extended tip and rounded to tapered, open to pinched lobes. Petiole pale glaucous gray-green. Flower pale lavender on an upright, bare, glaucous gray-green, 28 in. (70 cm) scape in high summer; fertility unknown.

Comments: Light to moderate shade. The leaf edge sometimes furls upward revealing the thickly powdered white back. Reasonably pest resistant.

Similar: *H.* 'Curls'.

Hosta 'Dancing in the Rain'

Large, medio-variegated leaves.

Clump size & habit: 49 in. wide × 28 in. high (122 × 70 cm). An upright mound.

Description: Leaf blade 11 × 9 in. (28 × 23 cm), very thick, ivory white, very irregularly margined and splashed blue-green turning dark green, with lighter green streaks jetting towards the midrib, matt above and glaucous below, seersuckered and puckered, widely veined, edge nearly flat, convex or cupped, almost round with heart-shaped folded to overlapping lobes. Petiole stout, white, outlined in blue-green. Flower bell-shaped, purple-striped lavender with a translucent margin, on an upright, bare, ivory, 36 in. (90 cm) scape in midsummer; fertile.

Comments: Morning sun in cooler climates helps increase vigor, but light to moderate shade produces a better contrast between the margin and the central variegation. The leaf center develops pale green frosting in extreme summer heat. Slow to start but needs regular division once established. Pest resistant. Zones 4–9.

Similar: *H.* 'American Masterpiece', *H.* 'Jim Wilkins', *H.* 'Northern Mystery'.

Hosta 'Dark Shadows'

Large, marginally variegated leaves.

Clump size & habit: 43½ in. wide × 20 in. high (109 × 50 cm). An open mound.

Description: Leaf blade 11 × 7½ in. (28 × 19 cm), of thick substance, emerging blue becoming greener, widely and irregularly margined chartreuse-yellow later turning green, matt above and glaucous below, gently ruffled, broadly oval with heart-shaped open lobes. Petiole dark blue-green. Flower fragrant, pale lavender with a translucent edge, on an upright, leafy, 27½ in. (69 cm) scape in midsummer; fertile. Zones 5–8.

Comments: Needs low light to achieve and retain its subtle leaf color contrasts and their changes through the summer. Best in cooler regions. Moderate to rapid growth rate.

Hosta 'Dark Star'

Small to medium, marginally variegated leaves.

Clump size & habit: 24 in. wide × 12 in. high (60 × 30 cm). A rippling mound.

Description: Leaf blade 7 × 3½ in. (18 × 9 cm), of average substance, smooth, dark green with a blue cast, irregularly margined ivory with some chartreuse streaking, satiny above and glaucous below, edge widely rippled, arching, narrowly oval with an acute tip and rounded, open lobes. Petiole olive green, finely outlined in ivory near the blade. Flower lavender on an upright, glaucous, red-dotted green, 18–24 in. (45–60 cm) scape in midsummer; fertile.

Comments: Light to full shade. Leaves widen with maturity so that young plants and mature plants look completely different. Rapid growth rate. Makes an excellent ground cover. Good in containers.

Similar: *H. kikutii* 'Kifukurin Hyuga', *H.* 'Shelleys'.

Sports: *H.* 'Darkest Star' (leaves narrow, ruffled, blue-green).

Hosta 'Dancing in the Rain'

Hosta 'Dark Shadows'

Hosta 'Dark Star', a mature clump.

Hosta 'Dawn's Early Light'

Hosta 'Dawn's Early Light'
Medium to large, yellowish leaves.

Clump size & habit: 36 in. wide × 20 in. high (90 × 50 cm). A pleasing symmetrical mound.

Description: Leaf blade 9 × 8 in. (23 × 20 cm), of average substance, matt pale yellow above, glaucous pale green below, prominently veined, seersuckered when mature, edge distinctly pie-crusted, convex and folded, nearly round with open to pinched lobes. Petiole narrowly channeled, chartreuse. Flower pale lavender on an upright, chartreuse, 29 in. (73 cm) scape in mid-summer; sterile.

Comments: Viridescent. Light to moderate shade where it will not scorch and will retain the exceptionally brilliant lemon-yellow leaf color in spring. A moderate to rapid grower. Lovely with early-flowering Japanese azaleas and *Heuchera* 'Obsidian'.

Similar: *H.* 'Abiqua Gold Shield', *H.* 'Sea Gulf Stream'.

Hosta 'Daybreak'
Large, yellowish leaves.

Clump size & habit: 60 in. wide × 12 in. high (150 × 30 cm). A wide, low mound of horizontal leaves.

Description: Leaf blade 14 × 10½ in. (35 × 26 cm), of thick substance, chartreuse-yellow turning deep golden yellow, shiny above and thinly glaucous below, veins closely ribbed, dimpled, edge shallowly undulate, slightly convex with heart-shaped pinched lobes. Petiole light chartreuse-yellow. Flower densely-packed, deep lavender-blue, on a pendant, leafy, dark green, 34 in. (85 cm) scape in mid to late summer; fertile.

Comments: Lutescent. Afternoon shade, particularly in hot climates. Among the best yellow-leaved hostas. Pest and weather resistant. Will light up dark borders.

Similar: *H.* 'Alice Gladden', *H.* 'Solar Flare' (leaves oval, more distinctly wavy).

Sports: *H.* 'Day's End' (leaves midgreen with an irregular golden yellow margin that widens considerably as the plant matures), *H.* 'Night Shift' (leaves dark green with a golden yellow margin).

Hosta 'Deane's Dream'
Medium, blue-green leaves.

Clump size & habit: 28 in. wide × 16 in. high (70 × 40 cm). An upright mound.

Description: Leaf blade 9 × 4 in. (23 × 10 cm), of thick substance, glaucous aquamarine to turquoise, edges slightly rippled, folded, widely oval with a graceful tip and tapered to heart-shaped, open to pinched lobes. Petiole narrowly channeled, bright purple. Flower pale lavender on an upright, glaucous blue, 22–26 in. (55–65 cm) scape in late summer; fertile.

Comments: Performs well in warmer climates but needs light to full shade all day. Moderate

Hosta 'Daybreak'

Hosta 'Deane's Dream'

growth rate. Grow at eye level to enjoy the attractive mauve petioles, which are more intensely purple-dotted than those of *H.* 'Venetian Blue' and are unusual in a hosta with this leaf color.

Similar: **H.* 'Blue Arrow', *H.* 'Hadspen Heron' (leaves more gray-green), **H.* 'Pineapple Poll'.

Hosta 'Deep Blue Sea'

Hosta 'Deep Blue Sea'

Small to medium, very blue leaves.

Clump size & habit: 30 in. wide × 13 in. high (75 × 33 cm). A stiff, open mound.

Description: Leaf blade 8 × 7½ in. (20 × 19 cm), very thick, emerging light green, soon becoming rich dark blue, intensely seersuckered and puckered, edge flat, distinctly cupped, nearly round with a vestigial tip and heart-shaped open lobes. Petiole coarse, flattish, pale green. Flower bell-shaped, rich lavender, in a dense raceme on an upright, bare, lilac-gray, 15 in. (38 cm) scape in high summer; fertile.

Comments: Good light to dappled shade. The leaves hold their superb blue color most of the summer; they are exaggeratedly rugose to seersuckered toward the central midrib, almost distorting the leaf symmetry, and lobes are sometimes twisted behind the petioles. Zones 3–7.

Similar: *H.* 'Willy Nilly'.

Hosta 'Dee's Golden Jewel'

Medium to large, yellowish leaves.

Hosta 'Dee's Golden Jewel'

Clump size & habit: 18 in. wide × 24 in. high (45 × 60 cm). An upright, rhizomatous mound.

Description: Leaf blade 6½ × 8½ in. (16 × 21 cm), very thick, chartreuse to golden yellow, matt above and glaucous below, veins ribbed, dimpled to seersuckered, edge rippled, folded or shallowly cupped, widely oval with a prominent tip and heart-shaped pinched lobes. Petiole chartreuse. Flower near-white in a dense raceme on a slightly leaning, leafy, chartreuse, 30 in. (75 cm) scape in midsummer; barely fertile.

Comments: Lutescent. Its sun tolerance, even in warm climates, and its heavy substance more than compensate for its less-than-spectacular leaf color. Very slow.

Sports: *H.* 'Bell Bottom Blues' (leaves an intense blue), *H.* 'Jewel of the Nile' (leaves blue-green with a yellow margin).

Hosta 'Deja Blu'

Small to medium, marginally variegated leaves.

Clump size & habit: 45½ in. wide × 15 in. high (114 × 38 cm). A low, cascading mound.

Description: Leaf blade 8 × 5 in. (20 × 13 cm), of average substance, soft glaucous blue-gray turning blue-green, irregularly margined in tricolor shades of chartreuse, narrowly outlined in cream with gray-green and cream streaking, smooth, attractively veined, edge slightly rippled, broadly oval with heart-shaped pinched to overlapping lobes. Petiole thin, pale blue-green. Flower pale lavender to near-white in profusion on an upright, leafy, pale green, 22 in. (55 cm) scape from early to midsummer; fertile.

Comments: Light shade. Vigorous, fast growing. The outstandingly unusual and attractive variegation takes several seasons to become fully apparent.

Similar: *H.* 'Bolt Out of the Blue', *H.* 'Rosedale Misty Pathways' (leaves larger), *H.* 'Toy Soldier'.

Hosta 'Devon Green'

Medium, green leaves.

Clump size & habit: 36 in. wide × 18 in. high (90 × 45 cm). A dense mound of overlapping leaves.

Hosta 'Deja Blu'

Hosta 'Devon Green'

Hosta 'Diamond Tiara'

Description: Leaf blade 7 × 4 in. (18 × 10 cm), of thick substance, smooth, glossy dark olive green, closely veined, edge flat, widely oval with an acute tip and heart-shaped pinched lobes. Petiole lighter olive green, with purple dots. Flower bell-shaped, near-white, in a dense raceme on a thick, upright, leafy, purple-tinged and -dotted olive green, 22½ in. (56 cm) scape in midsummer; fertile.

Comments: Light to moderate shade. Moderately fast growth rate. Lovely in a cream stone container. The best-selling green-leaved hosta in Europe.

Similar: *H.* 'Canadian Shield', **H.* 'Halcyon', *H.* 'Peridot', *H.* 'Valerie's Vanity'.

Sports: *H.* 'Silver Shadow'.

Hosta 'Diamond Tiara'

Small, marginally variegated leaves.

Clump size & habit: 25 in. wide × 14 in. high (63 × 35 cm). A spreading mound.

Description: Leaf blade 4½ × 3½ in. (11 × 9 cm), of thin substance, mid green with irregular pure white margins and some gray-green streaking, matt above and shiny below, some dimpling when mature, edge slightly rippled, slightly folded, widely oval with rounded, open to pinched lobes. Petiole green, outlined in white. Flower rich lavender in dense clusters on an upright, leafy, olive green, 22–25 in. (55–63 cm) scape in late summer; seedpods few; fertile.

Comments: Good light to moderate shade. Moderate to fast growing. An ideal edging plant and also good in pots. Zones 3–9.

Similar: *H.* 'Pearl Tiara', *H.* 'Touchstone'.

Hosta 'Diana Remembered'

Medium, marginally variegated leaves.

Clump size & habit: 24 in. wide × 15 in. high (60 × 38 cm). An open mound.

Description: Leaf blade 7 × 6½ in. (18 × 16 cm), of good substance, blue-green, widely and irregularly margined creamy white with transitional gray-green and chartreuse streaking, satiny above and matt below, widely veined, dimpled, edge slightly rippled, slightly cupped, widely oval

Hosta 'Diana Remembered'

Hosta 'Dick Ward'

Hosta 'Dorset Blue'

with heart-shaped pinched lobes. Petiole widely channeled, green with fine white lines, outlined in ivory. Flower 3 in. (8 cm) long, white, waxy, fragrant, on a stout, upright, leafy, green, 22 in. (55 cm) scape in late summer; fertile.

Comments: Sun for most of the day in cooler climates, morning sun only with plenty of moisture in hotter regions. Large, variegated bracts below the raceme. Rapid growth rate. A superb hosta with many attributes. Zones 3–9.

Similar: *H. plantaginea* 'Ming Treasure'.

Hosta 'Dick Ward'

Medium to large, medio-variegated leaves.

Clump size & habit: 40 in. wide × 18 in. high (100 × 45 cm). A dense mound.

Description: Leaf blade 9 × 9 in. (23 × 23 cm), of thick substance, glaucous, chartreuse-yellow turning golden yellow, irregularly margined dark green, seersuckered, edge wavy, cupped, widely oval to nearly round with a vestigial tip and heart-shaped open to pinched lobes. Petiole chartreuse, outlined in dark green. Flower pale lavender on an upright, chartreuse, leafy, 30 in. (75 cm) scape in mid to high summer; fertile.

Comments: Morning sun in cooler climates followed by good light to moderate shade in the afternoon. May become brassy yellow in strong sunlight. Slow to establish but well worth the wait. Pest resistant.

Similar: *H.* 'Midwest Magic' (leaf margin narrower and less intensely dark green), **H.* 'Paradigm', **H.* 'September Sun'.

Hosta 'Dorset Blue'

Small, very blue leaves.

Clump size & habit: 24 in. wide × 10 in. high (60 × 25 cm). An open mound.

Description: Leaf blade 4¾ × 4 in. (12 × 10 cm), of thick substance, glaucous intense bright blue with an attractive silver overlay, seersuckered, edge slightly undulate, cupped, heart-shaped to nearly round with a vestigial tip and heart-shaped pinched lobes. Petiole long, narrowly channeled, greenish blue. Flower bell-shaped, grayish white, in a dense raceme on an upright, bare, 14 in. (35 cm) scape in high to late summer; very fertile.

Comments: Dappled shade. Slow to increase. Pest resistant. A must-have for collectors of the bluest-leaved hostas. A superb breeding plant.

Similar: *H.* 'Blue Chip', **H.* 'Blue Moon', *H.* 'Gemstone' (among the most vigorous small blue-leaved hostas), **H.* 'Kiwi Blue Baby'.

Sports: *H.* 'Dorset Clown' (a popular breeding plant).

Hosta 'Dragon Tails'

Miniature, yellow leaves.

Clump size & habit: 8 in. high × 15 in. wide (20 × 38 cm). A low, dense mound.

Description: Leaf blade 4¾ × ¾ in. (12 × 2 cm), of thin substance, yellow, matt above and

Hosta 'Dragon Tails'

shiny below, veins closely ribbed, edge distinctly rippled, arching, lanceolate with an exaggeratedly extended tip, decurrent with an arching, narrowly channeled, pale chartreuse petiole. Flower lavender on an upright, bare, chartreuse, 10 in. (25 cm) scape in late summer; fertility unknown.

Comments: Lutescent. Suitable for warmer climates where it grows vigorously but needs shade. Rapid growth rate. Suitable for sinks or troughs or in a woodland border provided it is not smothered by larger plants.

Similar: *H.* 'Chartreuse Wiggles', *H.* 'Yellow Eyes', *H.* 'Yellow Ribbons', *H.* 'Yellow Waves'.

Hosta 'Eagle's Nest'

Large, marginally variegated leaves.

Clump size & habit: 30 in. wide × 18 in. high (75 × 45 cm). An impressive mound.

Description: Leaf blade 12 × 10 in. (30 × 25 cm), very thick, bright chartreuse to midgreen, widely margined and streaked yellow to cream, glossy above for part of the season and glaucous below, seersuckered and puckered, edge slightly undulate, deeply cupped, nearly round with a

Hosta 'Eagle's Nest'

vestigial tip and heart-shaped folded lobes. Petiole short, thick, green, outlined in cream. Flower pale lavender on a pendant, chartreuse, leafy, 44 in. (110 cm) scape in late summer; fertile.

Comments: Morning sun achieves the brightest color in cooler climates. Moderate growth rate. Pest resistant. Differs from most other *H.* 'Sum and Substance' sports in the smaller leaves with distinct cupping; somewhat slower growing. Blooms tightly clustered just above the foliage mound. Ideal for a subtropical border with *Miscanthus sinensis* 'Zebrinus' and the exotic spider daylily, *Hemerocallis* 'Yellow Angel'.

Similar: *H.* 'Lodestar' (leaf edge conspicuously rippled, leaf tip even more exaggerated).

Hosta 'Earth Angel'
Giant, marginally variegated leaves.

Clump size & habit: 61 in. wide × 36½ in. high (152 × 91 cm). A huge, undulating mound.

Description: Leaf blade 12 × 9 in. (30 × 23 cm), of thick substance, blue-green with wide pale green splashes, widely and irregularly margined and feathered yellow turning ivory white, matt above and glaucous below, veins closely ribbed, slight dimpling when mature, edge shallowly undulate, broadly oval to wedge-shaped with a pointed tip and heart-shaped pinched lobes. Petiole leaning, blue-green, outlined in cream. Flower long-lasting, palest lavender to near-white, in a dense raceme on an upright, leafy, blue-green, 48 in. (120 cm) scape in midsummer; fertility unknown.

Comments: Some morning sun in cooler regions, followed by light shade. Best as a specimen with space to increase over the years. Moderate growth rate. Pest resistant. Not suitable for containers. One of the largest and most outstanding cream-margined blue-leaved hostas.

Similar: *H.* 'Duke of Cornwall'.

Hosta 'El Capitan'
Large, marginally variegated leaves.

Clump size & habit: 42 in. wide × 24 in. high (105 × 60 cm). An open mound.

Description: Leaf blade 10½ × 9 in. (26 × 23 cm), of thick substance, dark sage green, widely and irregularly margined and streaked creamy yellow, matt above and powdery below, seersuckered and puckered, veins prominent, edge slightly undulate, kinked at the lobes, slightly arching or convex, oval to round with heart-shaped open to pinched lobes. Petiole dark

Hosta 'Earth Angel'

green, outlined in cream. Flower bell-shaped, rich mauve, opening from a gray-mauve bud, on an upright, bare, 34½ in. (86 cm) scape from mid to late summer; fertile.

Comments: Needs some morning sun in all but the hottest climates, where light to full shade best sets off the transitional gray-green streaking and misting. Rapid growth rate. Reasonably pest resistant. Use as a border specimen or for background planting. Lovely with blue-leaved hostas.

Similar: **H.* 'Carnival', *H.* 'Standing Ovation'.

Hosta 'El Niño'

Medium, marginally variegated leaves.

Clump size & habit: 30 in. wide × 20 in. high (75 × 50 cm). A graceful mound of attractively pointed leaves.

Description: Leaf blade 6 × 4½ in. (15 × 11 cm), of good substance, intense blue-gray, widely and irregularly margined white with gray-green streaking, matt above and glaucous below, closely veined, edge rippled, smooth, oval with heart-shaped open to pinched lobes. Peti-

ole blue-gray, narrowly outlined in white. Flower purple-striped lavender on an upright, leafy, glaucous blue-gray, 24 in. (60 cm) scape from mid to late summer; sterile.

Comments: Lowish light to dappled shade retains the best leaf color. Good in containers or at the margin of light woodland. Ideal where a pure white variegation is required.

Hosta 'El Capitan'

Hosta 'El Niño'

Hosta 'Electrum Stater'

Similar: **H.* 'Aristocrat', *H.* 'Chantilly Lace', *H.* 'Lacy Belle', *H.* 'Sleeping Beauty'.

Hosta 'Electrum Stater'

Medium, marginally variegated leaves.

Clump size & habit: 26 in. wide × 12 in. high (65 × 30 cm). A dense mound.

Description: Leaf blade 7½ × 6½ in. (19 × 16 cm), of thick substance, shiny chartreuse to bright golden yellow, irregularly margined creamy yellow turning pure white with some paler chartreuse streaking, seersuckered and puckered, edge slightly rippled, cupped or convex, widely oval to nearly round with heart-shaped overlapping lobes. Petiole chartreuse-yellow, outlined in cream. Flower palest lavender to near-white on an upright, leafy, chartreuse, 20 in. (50 cm) scape in late summer; fertile.

Comments: Takes sun all day except in the hottest regions. Prized for the three-tone effect of the leaves and margins and their color changes. Rapid growth rate. Pest resistant.

Similar: **H.* 'American Dream', *H.* 'Gaiety', *H.* 'Saint Elmo's Fire', *H.* 'Zodiac'.

Hosta 'Elvis Lives'

Medium, very blue leaves.

Clump size & habit: 36 in. wide × 18 in. high (90 × 45 cm). A moderately dense mound.

Description: Leaf blade 11 × 4½ in. (28 × 11 cm), of good substance, smooth, rich powdery blue, widely veined, edges distinctly rippled and twisted, arching toward the extended tip, lanceolate to oval with rounded, open lobes. Petiole blue-green. Flower long, lavender, on an upright, bare, light green, 22 in. (55 cm) scape in early to midsummer; fertile.

Comments: Dappled to light shade. Blue suedelike upper surface of the leaf will be apparent for longer in cooler climates. Moderate growth rate.

Similar: *H.* 'Venetian Blue', **H.* 'Winfield Blue'.

Hosta 'Emerald Necklace'

Medium, marginally variegated leaves.

Clump size & habit: 32½ in. wide × 16½ in. high (81 × 41 cm). A moderately dense, semi-upright mound.

Description: Leaf blade 5½ × 3½ in. (14 × 9 cm), of thick substance, chartreuse-white turning midgreen, widely and irregularly margined dark blue-green, satiny above and shinier below, closely veined, edge rippled, conspicuously twisted, oval with an acute tip and rounded pinched lobes. Petiole narrowly channeled, chartreuse to green. Flower violet-striped lavender on an upright, bare, olive green, 30 in. (75 cm) scape in late summer; fertile.

Comments: Not difficult to grow but careful siting between too much sun and too much shade is necessary to effect the interesting color changes. The conspicuously puckered margin and the transitional crimping between the margin and the leaf center give an embroidered effect. At its best in midsummer while the contrasting colors are at their height. Best as a foreground specimen or in a raised bed.

Similar: *H.* 'Collector's Banner', *H.* 'Embroidery'.

Sports: *H.* 'Ivory Necklace' (leaf margin cream).

Hosta 'Emerald Ruff Cut'

Medium, medio-variegated leaves.

Clump size & habit: 30 in. wide × 12 in. high (75 × 30 cm). A colorful cascading mound.

Description: Leaf blade 8 × 5 in. (20 × 13 cm), of good substance, bright golden yellow,

Hosta 'Elvis Lives'

Hosta 'Emerald Necklace'

Hosta 'Emerald Ruff Cut'

irregularly margined rich emerald green with some chartreuse streaking, veins closely ribbed, intensely seersuckered, edge rippled, wedge-shaped to oval with a long, pointed tip and heart-shaped pinched lobes. Petiole yellow, outlined in emerald green. Flower palest lavender on an upright, leafy, olive green, 20 in. (50 cm) scape in high summer; fertility unknown.

Comments: Best in cooler gardens in morning sun followed by light shade. Leaves reflush in midsummer. The seersuckering resembles blisters on the leaf surface, making this hosta quite distinct. Divide regularly.

Hosta 'Emerald Tiara'

Small, medio-variegated leaves.

Clump size & habit: 34 in. wide × 14 in. high (85 × 35 cm). A dense, spreading mound.

Hosta 'Emerald Tiara'

Description: Leaf blade 4½ × 3½ in. (11 × 9 cm), of average substance, smooth, muted gold, irregularly margined rich emerald green with some chartreuse streaking, widely veined, edge flat to occasionally kinked, widely oval with a vestigial tip and heart-shaped open to pinched lobes. Petiole chartreuse, outlined in emerald green. Flower rich lavender to purple in dense clusters on an upright, leafy, olive green, 22–25 in. (55–63 cm) scape in late summer; seedpods few; fertile.

Comments: Grow in some morning sun followed by good light to light shade in the afternoon. Leaf colors become more muted as the season progresses. Easy to grow. Divide frequently. A good foreground plant.

Similar: *H.* 'Emerald Scepter'.

Hosta 'Emily Dickinson'

Medium, marginally variegated leaves.

Clump size & habit: 41 in. wide × 18 in. high (102 × 45 cm). A dense mound.

Description: Leaf blade 6½ × 4 in. (16 × 10 cm), of average substance, smooth, medium green, widely and irregularly margined yellow turning creamy white with chartreuse streaking, satiny above and shiny below, edge slightly undulate, oval with an occasionally kinked, acute tip and rounded pinched lobes. Petiole green,

Hosta 'Emily Dickinson'

finely outlined in creamy white. Flower rich lavender on an upright, leafy, green, 28 in. (70 cm) scape in late summer; fertility unknown.

Comments: Some morning sun in cooler climates if moisture is available. Rapid growth rate.

Similar: *H.* 'Austin Dickinson', *H.* 'Bold Edger', *H.* 'Lacy Belle', **H.* 'Tambourine'.

Hosta 'English Sunrise'

Small to medium, yellowish leaves.

Clump size & habit: 30 in. wide × 16 in. high (75 × 40 cm). A mound of overlapping leaves.

Description: Leaf blade 5 × 3½ in. (13 × 9 cm), of thick substance, smooth, bright golden

Hosta 'English Sunrise'

yellow softening to chartreuse-green by midsummer but remaining bright in good light, matt above and glaucous below, edge slightly rippled, oval with a tiny tip and heart-shaped pinched lobes. Petiole chartreuse. Flower bell-shaped, near-white, in a dense raceme on a thick, upright, bare, mauve-gray, 22½ in. (56 cm) scape in midsummer; fertile.

Comments: Viridescent. The leaf remains yellow for longer if grown in morning sun. Needs careful siting to get the best from the available light.

Similar: *H.* 'Kiwi Gold Star', *H.* 'May', *H.* 'Prosperity'.

Hosta 'Fantabulous'

Medium to large, marginally variegated leaves.

Clump size & habit: 38½ in. wide × 26 in. high (96 × 65 cm). An upright mound.

Description: Leaf blade 9½ × 6 in. (24 × 15 cm), of good substance, dark spinach green, very widely and irregularly margined ivory white with gray-green streaking, satiny above and glossy below, widely veined, seersuckered, edge almost flat, lightly twisted, oval with a pointed tip and heart-shaped pinched to folded lobes. Petiole stout, streaked and margined white. Flower purple-striped lavender on an upright, leafy, dark green, 24 in. (60 cm) scape in midsummer; sterile.

Comments: Moderate shade as a specimen plant. Moderate growth rate. Lovely with *Brunnera* 'Langtrees' and silver-variegated asarums.

Similar: **H.* 'Liberty'.

Hosta 'Fire and Ice'

Medium, medio-variegated leaves.

Clump size & habit: 12 in. wide × 8 in. high (30 × 20 cm). An upright mound with twisted leaves.

Description: Leaf blade 6½ × 4 in. (16 × 10 cm), of good substance, smooth, creamy ivory to white, widely and irregularly margined dark green splashed several shades of green, satiny above and shiny below, edge kinked, lightly twisted and curved at the acute tip, widely oval with rounded, open lobes. Petiole ivory white, finely outlined in olive green. Flower pale lavender on an upright, leafy, white, 28 in. (70 cm) scape in high to late summer; seedpods white; poor fertility.

Hosta 'Fantabulous', a young plant.

Hosta 'Fire and Ice', showing a perfect balance of color.

Hosta 'Fire Island'

Comments: Bright light in the morning and avoid hot afternoon sun. Seemingly vigorous for a medio-variegated hosta.

Similar: *H.* 'Flash of Light', *H.* 'Loyalist', *H.* 'Paul Revere'.

Sports: *H.* 'Paradise on Fire' (leaves with a wide green margin and a narrow white center).

Hosta 'Fire Island'

Medium, yellowish leaves.

Clump size & habit: 34 in. wide × 14 in. high (85 × 35 cm). A dense mound.

Description: Leaf blade 6½ × 4½ in. (16 × 11 cm), of moderate substance, bright, pale acid-yellow turning chartreuse, shiny above and matt below, intensely seersuckered, edge distinctly rippled, widely oval with an elegant tip and flat to tapered, pinched lobes. Petiole intensely bright red-dotted and -streaked, this color persisting throughout the season. Flower lavender on an upright, leafy, chartreuse, 18–20 in. (45–50 cm) scape in late summer; fertile.

Comments: Viridescent. Shade all day. A rapid grower. Most effective when grown at eye level.

Similar: *H. longipes* 'Ogon Amagi'.

Hosta 'Fort Knox'

Large, yellowish leaves.

Clump size & habit: 43½ in. wide × 24 in. high (109 × 60 cm). An upright mound.

Description: Leaf blade 8½ × 5 in. (21 × 13 cm), of thick substance, chartreuse turning bright, clear yellow, satiny above and thinly glaucous below, seersuckered, edge flat to slightly kinked, folded, widely oval with a vestigial tip and heart-shaped pinched lobes. Petiole stout, chartreuse to olive green. Flower lavender on an upright, leafy, chartreuse-green, 30 in. (75 cm) scape in high to late summer; fertility unknown.

Comments: Lutescent. In cooler areas tolerates full sun all morning, elsewhere needs light to full shade all day. Many large bracts disposed around the raceme. Can easily exceed its registered dimensions. Moderate growth rate. Pest resistant.

Hosta 'Fort Knox'

Similar: *H.* 'Ultraviolet Light' (tolerates shorter periods of full sun).

Hosta 'Fortunei Aureomarginata'

Medium to large, marginally variegated leaves.

Clump size & habit: 51 in. wide × 22¾ in. high (127 × 57 cm). A dense mound.

Description: Leaf blade 8½ × 6½ in. (21 × 16 cm), of good substance, smooth, dark olive green, irregularly margined and streaked rich golden yellow turning cream, satiny above and thinly glaucous below, almost flat, slightly convex, oval with heart-shaped pinched lobes. Petiole olive green, outlined in creamy yellow. Flower 2 in. (5 cm) long, pale lavender, on an upright, leafy, green, 30 in. (75 cm) scape in high to late summer; marginally fertile.

Comments: Tolerates plenty of sun, although the leaf color will fade somewhat. Flower bracts below the blooms are ornamental even after flowering ceases. Vigorous, easy to grow. Ideal for covering large areas. A favorite of flower arrangers.

Hosta 'Fortunei Aureomarginata'

Similar: *H.* 'Anne', *H.* 'Ellerbroek', *H.* 'Royal Flush', *H.* 'Viette's Yellow Edge'.

Sports: *H.* 'Owen Online' (leaves with a central yellow stripe), *H.* 'Twilight' (leaves thicker).

Hosta 'Fortunei Hyacinthina'

Medium to large, gray-green leaves.

Clump size & habit: 45½ in. wide × 20 in. high (114 × 50 cm). A dense mound.

Description: Leaf blade 8½ × 6½ in. (21 × 16 cm), of good substance, dark gray-green turning green, thickly glaucous below, dimpled, edge slightly undulate with a hyaline line, slightly cupped, widely oval with heart-shaped pinched to overlapping lobes. Petiole dark green. Flower pinkish lavender, opening from a rich violet bud, in a dense raceme on an upright, leafy, glaucous green, 28 in. (70 cm) scape, purple-tinted toward the raceme, in high summer; poor fertility.

Comments: Adaptable. Tolerates morning sun, which enhances the already excellent flowers but causes the slight blueness in the leaves to disappear. Vigorous, fast growing. Grown primarily for its propensity to throw sports, the classic being *H.* 'Gold Standard'. The flowers have a fancied resemblance to those of hyacinth and are among the best in the genus.

Similar: *H.* 'Fortunei Rugosa'.

Sports: *H.* 'Alaskan Halo', *H.* 'Arctic Rim', **H.* 'Gold Standard', *H.* 'Heliarc', *H.* 'Julia'.

Hosta 'Fragrant Blue'

Medium, very blue leaves.

Clump size & habit: 36 in. wide × 15 in. high (90 × 38 cm). A dome-shaped mound.

Description: Leaf blade 8½ × 6½ in. (21 × 16 cm), of thick substance, smooth, powdery light blue, dimpled, edge almost flat, convex, widely oval with an elegant tip and heart-shaped open lobes. Petiole blue-green. Flower slightly fragrant, white, opening from a rich violet bud, on an upright, 30 in. (75 cm) scape in high summer; very fertile.

Comments: Good light to dappled shade needed to maintain the waxy coating. Vigorous. Among the few blue-leaved hostas with fragrant flowers, although the fragrance is only perceptible in hot climates.

Sports: **H.* 'Blue Flame' and *H.* 'Secret Love' (leaf margin creamy yellow).

Hosta 'Fortunei Hyachinthina'

Hosta 'Fragrant Bouquet'

Medium to large, marginally variegated leaves.

Clump size & habit: 26 in. wide × 18 in. high (65 × 45 cm). An open mound.

Description: Leaf blade 8½ × 6½ in. (21 × 16 cm), of moderate substance, chartreuse to pale green, widely margined yellow to creamy white with paler streaking, satiny above and thinly glaucous below, slightly dimpled, widely veined, edge shallowly undulate, convex, widely oval with heart-shaped open to pinched lobes. Petiole pale green, outlined in cream. Flower large, very fragrant, near-white, radially arranged, on an upright, pale green, 36 in. (90 cm) scape, with occasional large, variegated bracts toward the raceme, in late summer; usually sterile.

Comments: Full sun all day, except in the hottest climates, and moisture at the roots. Rapid growth rate. Named Hosta of the Year by the American Hosta Growers Association in 1998. Zones 3–9.

Similar: *H.* 'Crystal Moon', *H.* 'Sugar and Cream', *H.* 'Sweetie'.

Sports: *H.* 'Fragrant Dream' (leaves darker green with a darker yellow margin), **H.* 'Guacamole'.

Hosta 'Fragrant Blue'

Hosta 'Fragrant Bouquet'

Hosta 'Francee'

Medium to large, marginally variegated leaves.

Clump size & habit: 51 in. wide × 21 in. high (127 × 53 cm). A dense mound.

Description: Leaf blade 8½ × 5 in. (21 × 13 cm), of average substance, dark green, crisply and narrowly margined white with gray-green streaking, matt above and glaucous below, dimpled when mature, edge almost flat, widely oval, with heart-shaped open or folded lobes. Petiole dark green, outlined in white. Flower pale lavender on an upright, leafy, green, 28 in. (70 cm) scape in high to late summer; poor fertility.

Comments: Morning sun except in the hottest climates, but the leaf color fades to palest olive green. Distinctive, bright purple shoots emerge very late. The narrowly funnel-shaped flowers do not always open at the tips of the scapes. Superb in a large container and also excellent for land-

Hosta 'Francee'

Hosta 'Frosted Jade'

scaping since it is a rapid grower. It is a sport of *H.* 'Fortunei Albomarginata'. Zones 3–9.

Similar: *H.* 'Carol', *H.* 'Fortunei Albomarginata', *H.* 'North Hills', *H.* 'Rhino', *H.* 'Zager's White Edge'.

Sports: *H.* 'Academy Fire' (leaves emerge yellow turning light green), *H.* 'Jade Beauty', *H.* 'Minuteman', *H.* 'Pathfinder' (leaves occasionally with a misted effect in the center), **H.* 'Patriot', *H.* 'The Matrix' (central leaf variegation emerges golden yellow becoming white-flecked with green), *H.* 'Trailblazer' (leaves dark green with a contrasting wide, creamy white margin).

Hosta 'Frosted Jade'

Large to giant, marginally variegated leaves.

Clump size & habit: 60 in. wide × 28–32 in. high (150 × 70–80 cm). An upright, arching mound.

Description: Leaf blade 14 × 10 in. (35 × 25 cm), of good substance, dark sage green, narrowly and irregularly margined pure white with some gray-green streaking, matt above and thinly glaucous below, strongly veined, edge closely rippled and slightly upturned, oval with heart-shaped pinched lobes. Petiole deeply channeled, green, outlined in white. Flower near-white in a dense raceme on a leaning, leafy, green, 40 in. (100 cm) scape in midsummer; fertile, producing abundant seed.

Comments: Light to moderate shade. Use as a specimen or at the edge of a woodland.

Similar: *H. montana* 'Mountain Snow', *H. montana* 'Summer Snow', *H. montana* 'White On', *H.* 'Snow Crust'.

Hosta 'Frozen Margarita'

Large, marginally variegated leaves.

Clump size & habit: 40 in. wide × 18 in. high (100 × 45 cm). An open, arching mound.

Description: Leaf blade 8 × 6 in. (20 × 15 cm), of leathery substance, glossy golden yellow, narrowly and irregularly margined pure white, widely veined, moderately seersuckered, edge flat, broadly oval with a recurved tip and pinched to folded lobes. Petiole long, chartreuse-green, narrowly outlined in white. Flower large, radially

arranged, fragrant palest lavender to pearlescent white on a slightly arching to upright, large, leafy, chartreuse-gold, 33½ in. (84 cm) scape in late summer; some seeds fertile.

Comments: Tolerates sun all day except in the hottest climates given sufficient moisture. Ideal in containers in cooler gardens, sited to appreciate the fragrance of the superb flowers. Rapid growth rate.

Similar: *H.* 'Joshua's Banner'.

Hosta 'Gemini Moon'

Medium, marginally variegated leaves.

Clump size & habit: 40 in. wide × 20 in. high (100 × 50 cm). A dense, somewhat asymmetrical mound.

Hosta 'Frozen Margarita'

Hosta 'Gemini Moon'

Description: Leaf blade 8 × 7½ in. (20 × 19 cm), of good substance, matt dark green, very widely and irregularly margined chartreuse becoming soft yellow then glowing golden yellow with chartreuse streaking, veins strongly marked, seersuckered and puckered, edge slightly undulate, mature leaves slightly convex, widely oval to nearly round with heart-shaped open to pinched lobes. Petiole dark green, outlined in yellow. Flower large, bell-shaped, soft lavender to near-white, on an upright, leafy, glaucous green, 25 in. (63 cm) scape in high summer; fertile.

Comments: Suitable for hotter climates if sited in light shade but enjoys some morning sun in cooler gardens. Vigorous. Moderate growth rate. Sometimes throws all-yellow leaves which should be removed to prevent reversion. Grow with ferns or blue-leaved hostas.

Similar: *H.* 'Abiqua Moonbeam' (leaf margin narrower, leaf color less pronounced).

Hosta 'Gentle Giant'

Giant, bluish leaves.

Clump size & habit: 68 in. wide × 45½ in. high (170 × 114 cm). A huge, upright mound.

Description: Leaf blade 13 × 12 in. (33 × 30 cm), of thick substance, leathery, intensely glaucous blue-green, veins prominent and widely spaced, dimpled, edge flat, cupped, moderately twisted and folded. Petiole very deeply channeled, pale frosted green. Flower 2¾ in. (7 cm) long, lavender, on an upright, leafy, frosted green, 49–58 in. (122–147 cm) scape in midsummer; very fertile.

Comments: Sun tolerant in cooler climates, although strong sunlight melts the wax off the leaves angled directly at its rays turning them green; leaves in the shade are not affected. If sited in shade, the leaves hold their blue color all summer. Best not planted immediately under trees as falling debris will collect in the deeply cupped leaves. The leafy bracts are small. One of

Hosta 'Gentle Giant'

the largest hostas with blue leaves. Rapid growth rate. Pest resistant.

Hosta 'Ginko Craig'

Small to medium, marginally variegated leaves.

Clump size & habit: 44½ in. wide × 14 in. high (112 × 35 cm). A dense, spreading mound.

Description: Leaf blade 5 × 2½ in. (13 × 6 cm), of thin substance, dark green, crisply margined pure white with gray-green streaking, matt above and slightly shiny below, dimpled when mature, edge rippled, arching, slightly convex, elliptic with an acute tip and tapered, open lobes. Petiole shallowly channeled, green, outlined in white. Flower dark purple-striped purple on an upright, bare, green, 22 in. (55 cm) scape from late summer to early autumn; very fertile.

Comments: Light to moderate shade. The supreme edging hosta. Vigorous and easy to grow. The narrow, rippled, lanceolate juvenile leaf blades differ significantly from the mature elliptic to oval ones.

Similar: H. 'Allen P. McConnell', H. 'Blade Runner', H. 'Bunchoko', H. 'Excalibur', H. 'Ground Master', H. 'Little Wonder', H. 'Peedee Laughing River', H. 'Princess of Karafuto'.

Sports: H. 'Hi Ho Silver', H. 'Sarah Kennedy' (leaf margin significantly wider).

Hosta 'Glacier Cascade'

Large, green leaves.

Clump size & habit: 36 in. wide × 26 in. high (90 × 65 cm). A cascading mound.

Description: Leaf blade 10¾ × 4½ in. (27 × 11 cm), of average substance, light olive green, matt above and thickly glaucous below, closely veined, edge widely and evenly rippled, slightly twisted to moderately wavy, lanceolate with an elongated acute tip and tapered, open lobes. Petiole narrowly channeled, olive green. Flower lavender-striped near-white, reflexed at the tip,

Hosta 'Ginko Craig'

on a leaning, leafy, light green, 30 in. (75 cm) scape in midsummer; seedpods green; fertile.

Comments: Light to moderate shade. Moderate growth rate. A hosta with great presence.

Hosta 'Gold Edger'

Small to medium, yellowish leaves.

Clump size & habit: 25 in. wide × 9–12 in. high (63 × 23–30 cm). A dense, symmetrical mound.

Description: Leaf blade 3½ × 2½ in. (9 × 6 cm), of thick substance, muted golden yellow fading to chartreuse, matt to glaucous above and glaucous below, dimpled, edge sometimes kinked, cupped, widely oval with heart-shaped overlapping lobes. Petiole narrowly channeled, chartreuse. Flower bell-shaped, lavender, on a leaning to upright, bare, chartreuse, 12 in. (30 cm) scape in late summer; fertile.

Comments: Viridescent. Usually exceeds registered dimensions. Leaf color is very dependent

Hosta 'Glacier Cascade'

Hosta 'Gold Edger'

on the light quality. Tolerates full sun all day except in hotter climates. A popular edging plant. Zones 3–9.

Similar: *H.* 'Birchwood Parky's Gold', *H.* 'Gold Drop'.

Sports: *H.* 'Hawkeye' (leaf margin golden yellow), *H.* 'June Bug' (leaf margin green), *H.* 'Olympic Edger' (leaves chartreuse with an ivory margin), *H.* 'Radiant Edger' (leaves green with a chartreuse margin), *H.* 'Timothy' (leaves green with a muted yellow margin).

Hosta 'Gold Regal'

Large to giant, yellowish leaves.

Clump size & habit: 51 in. wide × 36 in. high (127 × 90 cm). A semi-upright, dense mound of overlapping leaves.

Hosta 'Gold Regal'

Description: Leaf blade 8½–11 × 7½–8½ in. (21–28 × 19–21 cm), of thick substance, chartreuse to old-gold, matt above and thickly glaucous below, veins deeply impressed, dimpled, edge flat, slightly folded, widely oval with tapered, pinched lobes. Petiole stout, glaucous chartreuse. Flower large, bell-shaped, grayish mauve, on a stout, leafy, upright, glaucous green, 30–39 in. (75–98 cm) scape in midsummer; fertile.

Comments: Lutescent. Superb flowers are only one of this hosta's many attributes. Tolerates long exposure to sun in most regions, but only morning sun in the hottest climates. Pest resistant. Leaves remain chartreuse if grown in shade all day.

Similar: *H.* 'Golden Torch', *H.* 'Ultraviolet Light'.

Sports: **H.* 'Alex Summers', *H.* 'David Reath' (leaves dark green with a yellow margin), *H.* 'Independence Day' (leaves pale green with a muted yellow margin), *H.* 'Rascal'.

Hosta 'Gold Standard'

Medium to large, medio-variegated leaves.

Clump size & habit: 41 in. wide × 22 in. high (102 × 55 cm). A dense mound of overlapping leaves.

Description: Leaf blade 8½ × 5½ in. (21 × 14 cm), of good substance, chartreuse, turn-

Hosta 'Gold Standard'

ing yellow then ivory, irregularly margined dark green with some chartreuse streaking, matt above and glaucous below, seersuckered, edge slightly rippled, slightly cupped, widely oval with heart-shaped pinched to overlapping lobes. Petiole chartreuse, outlined in dark green. Flower pinkish lavender, opening from a rich violet bud, in a dense raceme on an upright, leafy, glaucous green, 28 in. (70 cm) scape, purple-tinted toward the raceme, in high summer; poor fertility.

Comments: Albescent. Very sensitive to light levels. Bright light to moderate shade, depending on summer heat and the leaf color required.

Hosta 'Golden Prayers'

Hosta 'Golden Sculpture'

Emerges late from purple shoots. Vigorous and easy to grow. A colorful specimen in the border and excellent in containers. Winner of the 1993 Alex J. Summers Distinguished Merit Hosta Award. Has probably produced more worthwhile sports than any other hosta. Divide regularly. Zones 3–9.

Similar: *H.* 'Janet'.

Sports: *H.* 'Academy Muse' (leaves with a subtle, darker green margin when grown in full shade and a gold center with a green margin and green veins when grown in partial sun), **H.* 'Brenda's Beauty', **H.* 'Captain Kirk', *H.* 'Collector's Banner', *H.* 'Darwin's Standard', *H.* 'Gypsy Rose' (leaves with no transitional white marking), **H.* 'Kiwi Full Monty', *H.* 'Moonlight',

H. 'Paradise Standard', *H.* 'Richland Gold', *H.* 'Something Different', *H.* 'String Bikini' (leaves very narrow), **H.* 'Striptease'.

Hosta 'Golden Prayers'

Medium, yellowish leaves.

Clump size & habit: 16–18 in. wide × 9½–12 in. high (40–45 × 24–30 cm). An upright mound.

Description: Leaf blade 8 × 6½ in. (20 × 16 cm), of thick substance, glaucous, chartreuse turning golden yellow, intensely seersuckered with occasional puckering, edge almost flat, deeply cupped or folded, widely oval with a vestigial tip and rounded pinched lobes. Petiole chartreuse to yellow. Flower near-white on an upright, bare, yellow, 20 in. (50 cm) scape in midsummer; fertility uncertain.

Comments: Lutescent. Needs shade all day to avoid scorching the leaf edge. Slow to moderate growth rate. Pest resistant.

Similar: *H.* 'Golden Bullion', *H.* 'Golden Medallion', *H.* 'Golden Waves', **H.* 'King Tut', *H.* 'Thai Brass'.

Hosta 'Golden Sculpture'

Large, yellowish leaves.

Clump size & habit: 50 in. wide × 26 in. high (125 × 65 cm). A vase-shaped mound.

Description: Leaf blade 11 × 10 in. (28 × 25 cm), of thick substance, sharp chartreuse-yellow fading to lighter yellow, thinly glaucous, evenly seersuckered, edge widely undulate, convex when mature, slightly arching at the distinctive tip, widely oval with heart-shaped overlapping lobes. Petiole chartreuse. Flower near-white in a dense raceme on an upright, leafy, green, 41 in. (102 cm) scape in midsummer; fertile.

Comments: Lutescent. Best with some morning sun in cooler climates, elsewhere shade all day to prevent scorching. The midrib and veins remain green. Slow growth rate but worth the wait, eventually exceeding its registered dimensions. Pest resistant. Winner of the 1991 Alex J. Summers Distinguished Merit Hosta Award.

Similar: **H.* 'Fort Knox', *H.* 'High Noon'.

Sports: *H.* 'Garden Party' (leaf margin narrow and green).

Hosta 'Golden Teacup'

Small, yellowish leaves.

Clump size & habit: 18 in. wide × 12 in. high (45 × 30 cm). An upright mound.

Description: Leaf blade 4¾ × 4½ in. (12 × 11 cm), of thick substance, bright yellow turning chartreuse, matt above and glaucous below, intensely seersuckered, edge flat, folded to deeply cupped, widely oval to round with heart-shaped pinched to overlapping lobes. Petiole narrowly channeled, chartreuse. Flower white on an upright, bare, 12 in. (30 cm) scape from mid to late summer; fertile.

Comments: Viridescent. Provide some morning sun for the golden leaf color to remain longer. Slow but worth the wait as the leaves develop an attractive shape and surface texture. Pest resistant.

Hosta 'Golden Teacup'

Hosta 'Golden Tiara'

Small to medium, marginally variegated leaves.

Clump size & habit: 38¾ in. wide × 16 in. high (97 × 40 cm). A spreading mound.

Description: Leaf blade 5 × 4½ in. (13 × 11 cm), of moderate substance, midgreen, irregularly margined chartreuse turning yellow then fading to cream with chartreuse streaking, matt above and shiny below, dimpled when mature, edge slightly rippled, widely oval with heart-shaped open to pinched lobes. Petiole olive green, outlined in cream. Flower rich lavender to purple in dense clusters on an upright, leafy, olive green, 22–25 in. (55–63 cm) scape in late summer; seedpods few; fertile.

Comments: Good light to light shade. Rapid growth, soon exceeding its registered dimensions. Leaves vary in shape, the outer ones being oval, the inner ones sometimes almost round. Flowers turn darker purple when exposed to sunlight. Some rebloom if spent scapes are removed. Among the most important hostas ever introduced. Winner of the 1994 Alex J. Summers Distinguished Merit Hosta Award. Zones 3–9.

Hosta 'Golden Tiara'

Similar: *H.* 'Grand Tiara'.

Sports: **H.* 'Diamond Tiara', *H.* 'Emerald Scepter', *H.* 'Golden Scepter', *H.* 'Jade Scepter', *H.* 'Platinum Tiara', *H.* 'Ribbon Tiara', *H.* 'Royal Tiara'.

Hosta 'Grand Slam'

Small to medium, green leaves.

Clump size & habit: 26½ in. wide × 10 in. high (66 × 25 cm). A dome-shaped rippled mound.

Description: Leaf blade 7 × 6½ in. (18 × 16 cm), very leathery, dark olive green, shiny above and thickly glaucous below, slightly dimpled, edge distinctly and evenly rippled, flat, heart-

Hosta 'Grand Slam'

Hosta 'Great Lakes Gold'

Hosta 'Great Plains'

shaped with a long thin tip and heart-shaped overlapping lobes. Petiole narrowly channeled, purple-tinted green. Flower funnel-shaped, rich violet, on an upright, leafy, purple, 20½ in. (51 cm) scape in early to mid autumn; fertile.

Comments: Good pollen parent for leaf substance and shape. Grow at eye level for best effect in light to moderate shade. Pest resistant.

Similar: *H.* 'One Man's Treasure'.

Hosta 'Great Lakes Gold'

Large, yellowish leaves.

Clump size & habit: 67 in. wide × 22 in. high (168 × 55 cm). An open, tiered mound.

Description: Leaf blade 12 × 10 in. (30 × 25 cm), of good substance, matt chartreuse turning golden yellow, veins furrowed, dimpled, edge distinctly and attractively rippled, arching toward the elegant tip, oval with deeply heart-shaped open to pinched lobes. Petiole stout, yellow. Flower pale lavender on an upright, leafy, green, 27–29 in. (68 to 73 cm) scape in early summer; fertile.

Comments: Lutescent. Grow in morning sun everywhere except the hottest climates to maintain the leaf color. Provide plenty of moisture. One of the very few large, golden yellow hostas having rippled edges. Pest resistant.

Similar: *H.* 'Jimmy Crack Corn'.

Hosta 'Great Plains'

Large to giant, blue-gray leaves.

Clump size & habit: 41½ in. wide × 25 in. high (104 × 63 cm). A semi-upright mound.

Description: Leaf blade 16 × 12 in. (40 × 30 cm), of thick substance, gray-blue, veins furrowed, edge rippled to piecrusted, undulate, widely oval with heart-shaped open lobes. Petiole stout, light green. Flower long, pale lavender, in a dense raceme on an upright or leaning, leafy, blue-green, 41½ in. (104 cm) scape from mid to high summer; fertile.

Comments: Dappled to moderate shade. Upper leaf surface soon loses its waxy coating becoming blue-green, finally dark green; the underside remains a light glaucous blue. Pest resistant.

Similar: *H.* 'Grey Piecrust'.

Hosta 'Great River Sonata'

Large, marginally variegated leaves.

Clump size & habit: 51 in. wide × 24 in. high (127 × 60 cm). An open mound.

Description: Leaf blade 11 × 9 in. (28 × 23 cm), of thick substance, leathery, green-gray with slight blue cast which fades later, narrowly and irregularly margined ivory, satiny above and glaucous below, smooth, edge shallowly undulate, flat, widely veined, broadly oval with a pointed tip and round, pinched to folded lobes. Petiole dark green, finely outlined in ivory. Flower large, fragrant, violet-flushed pale lavender, on a leaning, leafy, green, 18 in. (45 cm) scape from late summer to early autumn; fertility unknown.

Comments: Best in cooler climates in shade. Pest resistant. The blue-toned leaves gradually turn green, and the variegated margins are an added enhancement to its superb plain-leaved parent *H.* 'Moonlight Sonata'; the heavy flower trusses are a bonus especially if grown with blue asters and colchicums, providing a delightful sight in the autumn garden. Alternatively contrast it with **H.* 'Fire Island' whose harsh golden leaves and red petioles will create a lively picture.

Hosta 'Green Fountain'

Medium to large, green leaves.

Clump size & habit: 56 in. wide × 16 in. high (140 × 40 cm). A cascading mound.

Hosta 'Great River Sonata'

Hosta 'Green Fountain'

Description: Leaf blade 12 × 3½ in. (30 × 9 cm), of moderately thick substance, smooth, olive green, shiny above and very glossy below, veins prominent and widely spaced, edge heavily rippled, oblong to elliptic, pinched just above the recurved tip, lobes tapered and pinched. Petiole green with red streaks. Flower in a large lilac truss on a drooping, leafy, intensely red-streaked green, 51 in. (127 cm) scape in late summer; fertile.

Comments: Light to moderate shade all day. A graceful hosta, best cascading down walls or from terracotta chimney pots, but also valuable for its showy late flowers.

Similar: *H. kikutii* 'Caput Avis'.

Sports: *H.* 'Fountain of Youth' (leaf margin white), *H.* 'Three Coins' (leaves midgreen with a pale yellow margin).

Hosta 'Guacamole'

Large, medio-variegated leaves.

Clump size & habit: 51 in. wide × 24 in. high (127 × 60 cm). A mound of overlapping leaves.

Description: Leaf blade 11 × 8½ in. (28 × 21 cm), of good substance, chartreuse turning dull-gold, irregularly margined dark green with chartreuse streaking, glossy above and thinly glaucous below, widely veined, edge almost flat, slightly convex, widely oval with heart-shaped pinched to overlapping lobes. Petiole chartreuse, faintly outlined in dark green. Flower

Hosta 'Guacamole', leaves

Hosta 'Guacamole', flower

large, fragrant, near-white, radially arranged, on an upright, pale green, 36 in. (90 cm) scape, with occasional large, variegated bracts toward the raceme, in late summer; usually sterile.

Comments: Full sun all day in cooler climates, elsewhere morning sun. The margin is barely visible in cooler climates even if exposed to sunlight. Rapid growth rate. Named Hosta of the Year by the American Hosta Growers Association in 2002. Zones 3–9.

Sports: *H.* 'Avocado', *H.* 'Fried Green Tomatoes' (leaves dark green), **H.* 'Holy Molé', *H.* 'Paradise Sunshine', *H.* 'Stained Glass' (leaves vivid yellow with a narrow dark green margin).

Hosta 'Guardian Angel'

Large giant, medio-variegated leaves.

Clump size & habit: 36 in. wide × 24 in. high (90 × 60 cm). A moderately dense mound.

Description: Leaf blade 16 × 10 in. (40 × 25 cm), of thick substance, emerging greenish white turning light blue-green and finally midgreen, widely and irregularly margined dark blue-green

with chartreuse streaking, matt above and glaucous below, dimpled when mature, veins prominent, edge conspicuously rippled, folded, widely oval with heart-shaped overlapping lobes. Petiole chartreuse-white. Flower long lasting, palest lavender to near-white, in a dense raceme on a stout, upright, leafy, gray-green, 48 in. (120 cm) scape in midsummer; fertile.

Comments: Viridescent. Grow in light shade. The twisting of the leaf is most apparent in young plants; the leaves flatten and expand with maturity. Variegation is not visible on the second flush of leaves. Zones 4–8.

Similar: *H.* 'Angel Eyes'.

Hosta 'Gunsmoke'

Giant, grayish blue leaves.

Clump size & habit: 65 in. wide × 30½ in. high (163 × 76 cm). An impressive, arching mound.

Description: Leaf blade 14 × 10 in. (35 × 25 cm), leathery, emerging light blue-green and gradually turning a rich deep blue-green with a

Hosta 'Guardian Angel'

grayish cast, satiny above and glaucous below, prominently and widely veined, seersuckered, edge shallowly undulate, flat, broadly oval to rounded with a long thin tip and pinched to overlapping lobes. Petiole blue-green. Flower lavender on an almost horizontal, leafy, 36 in.

Hosta 'Gunsmoke'

(90 cm) scape from late spring to midsummer; seedpods green; fertility unknown.

Comments: Light to moderate shade. Useful as a background plant or a single specimen. Vigorous. Pest resistant.

Hosta 'Hadspen Blue'

Medium, very blue leaves.

Clump size & habit: 34½ in. wide × 18½ in. high (86 × 46 cm). An open mound.

Description: Leaf blade 7 × 6½ in. (18 × 16 cm), of thick substance, smooth rich blue, some dimpling when mature, edge almost flat, slightly cupped or convex, heart-shaped to nearly round with heart-shaped overlapping lobes. Petiole stout, pale blue-gray. Flower bell-shaped, lavender-gray to near-white, on an upright, bare, glaucous gray-blue, 18 in. (45 cm) scape in mid to high summer; fertile.

Comments: Needs shade all day. Does not form a symmetrical mound, but the wonderful

Hosta 'Hadspen Blue'

leaf color holds for longer than most others, making this a very worthwhile garden plant. Early to emerge. Slow growing. Pest resistant.

Similar: *H.* 'Happiness'.

Sports: **H.* 'Aristocrat'.

Hosta 'Halcyon'

Medium, blue leaves.

Clump size & habit: 41 in. wide × 18 in. high (102 × 45 cm). A symmetrical mound.

Description: Leaf blade 6½ × 4 in. (16 × 10 cm), of thick substance, smooth, intense glaucous blue, edge almost flat, widely oval with a pointed tip and heart-shaped pinched to overlapping lobes. Petiole flattish, blue-green. Flower bell-shaped, near-white, in a dense raceme on a thick, upright, bare, mauve-gray, 22 in. (55 cm) scape in midsummer; fertile.

Comments: Holds its color well into late summer given good light to dappled shade. Juvenile leaves are conspicuously narrow, especially in micropropagated plants. Superb in a container. Winner of the 1987 Alex J. Summers Distinguished Merit Hosta Award.

Similar: *H.* 'Devon Mist'.

Sports: *H.* 'Canadian Shield', **H.* 'Devon Green', *H.* 'Peridot', and *H.* 'Valerie's Vanity' (leaves dark green); *H.* 'First Frost' and *H.* 'Sleeping Beauty' (leaf margin creamy white); *H.* 'Goldbrook Glimmer' (leaves a muted chartreuse to old gold with a wide rich blue margin); **H.* 'June'.

Hosta 'Hanky Panky'

Small to medium, medio-variegated leaves.

Clump size & habit: 33½ in. high × 13 in. wide (84 × 33 cm). A strikingly variegated mound.

Description: Leaf blade 7 × 3 in. (18 × 8 cm), of average substance, matt dark green, widely and irregularly margined pale chartreuse-green with a randomly marked silver-white halo separating the margin from the center, seersuckered, oval with a

Hosta 'Halcyon'

Hosta 'Hanky Panky'

Hosta 'Harpoon'

pointed tip and tapered, open to pinched lobes. Petiole dark green, outlined in chartreuse. Flower pinkish lavender, opening from a rich violet bud, in a dense raceme on an upright, leafy, green, 23 in. (58 cm) scape, purple-tinted towards the raceme, in high summer; sterile.

Comments: Needs good light to dappled shade for optimum leaf color which is most outstanding in early summer when the white halo is clearly visible. The leaf gradually turns creamy yellow and the margin ivory with a pale green overlay; some dark green is retained, mostly toward the tip. Excellent in containers. Vigorous, fast growing. The complex variegation may disappear unless the plant is frequently divided.

Hosta 'Harpoon'

Medium, marginally variegated leaves.

Clump size & habit: 24 in. wide × 14 in. high (60 × 35 cm). An open mound.

Description: Leaf blade 11 × 3½ in. (28 × 9 cm), of average substance, mid to dark green, glossy above and satiny below, irregularly margined and streaked cream, dimpled, widely and prominently veined, edge unevenly rippled, arching, shallowly undulate, lanceolate to oval with a pointed tip and tapered, open to pinched lobes. Petioles narrowly channeled, green, finely edged yellow to cream. Flower spider-shaped, violet with contrasting white center, widely spaced on an upright, green, leafy, 40 in. (100 cm) scape from mid to late summer; fertility unknown.

Comments: Morning sun followed by light shade. Vigorous. The margin fades from golden yellow to cream. A multi-award winner. Zones 3–9.

Similar: *H.* 'Cordelia', *H.* 'Don Stevens'.

Hosta 'Harry van der Laar'

Medium, green leaves.

Clump size & habit: 24 in. wide × 12 in. high (60 × 30 cm). An upright, open mound.

Description: Leaf blade 7½ × 5 in. (19 × 13 cm), of good substance, midgreen, smooth above and thickly glaucous below, widely veined, edge undulate, oval with an elegant tip and rounded to flat lobes. Petiole intensely claret-pink dotted. Flower lavender on an upright, leafy, gray-green, 16 in. (40 cm) scape in late summer; fertility unknown.

Comments: Light to moderate shade. Grow at eye level to enjoy the white leaf backs and the strikingly colored petioles. The leaf bases are also red-dotted. Moderate growth rate. Zones 4–8.

Similar: *H.* 'Marilyn Monroe'.

Hosta 'High Society'

Small to medium, medio-variegated leaves.

Clump size & habit: 24 in. wide × 12 in. high (60 × 30 cm). A dome-shaped dense mound.

Description: Leaf blade 5½ × 4½ in. (14 × 11 cm), of thick substance, glaucous chartreuse to golden yellow, fading to ivory, very widely and

Hosta 'Harry van der Laar'

Hosta 'High Society'

Hosta 'Holy Molé'

irregularly margined intense blue-green with chartreuse streaking, edge almost flat, closely veined, smooth, cupped, broadly oval with a pointed tip and heart-shaped pinched to folded lobes. Petiole chartreuse to ivory, outlined in blue-green. Flower bell-shaped, near-white, in a dense raceme on a stout, upright, bare, light green, 18 in. (45 cm) scape in midsummer; seedpods blue-green; fertility unknown.

Comments: Light to moderate shade. Slow growing. Superb in containers, attractive for the whole season. Simple, elegant containers accentuate the dramatic variegation. Pest resistant. Differs from its parent *H.* 'June' in having a more upright habit and in having leaves which are more vividly colored and more prominently veined. Divide regularly.

Similar: *H.* 'Grand Marquee', *H.* 'Touch of Class'.

Hosta 'Holy Molé'

Large, medio-variegated leaves.

Clump size & habit: 42¾ in. wide × 24 in. high (107 × 60 cm). A dome-shaped, dense mound.

Description: Leaf blade 11 × 9 in. (28 × 23 cm), of thick substance, rubbery, chartreuse, very widely and irregularly margined dark green with dark green and chartreuse streaking, shiny above and glaucous below, dimpled, convex, nearly round with heart-shaped pinched lobes. Petiole chartreuse, outlined in dark green. Flower large, fragrant, near-white, radially arranged, on an upright, pale green, 36 in. (90 cm) scape, with

Hosta 'Honeybells'

occasional large variegated bracts toward the raceme, in late summer; usually sterile.

Comments: Full sun all day, except in the hottest regions, to produce the most prolific display of flowers; abundant moisture at the roots is essential. Increases rapidly. Divide frequently. Zones 3–9.

Similar: *H.* 'Avocado', **H.* 'Cathedral Windows'.

Hosta 'Honeybells'

Medium to large, marginally variegated leaves.

Clump size & habit: 51 in. wide × 26½ in. high (127 × 66 cm). A lax mound.

Description: Leaf blade 10 × 6½ in. (25 × 16 cm), of thinnish substance, light olive green, satiny to glossy above and shiny below, widely veined, edge shallowly undulate, arching to drooping from the base, oval with rounded, open to pinched lobes. Petiole narrowly channeled, light olive green. Flower slightly fragrant, palest lavender, on an upright, leafy, green, 45 in. (113 cm) scape from late summer to early autumn; fertile.

Comments: Tolerates full sun, which brings out its elusive fragrance. Flowers open as the temperature rises, but the leaves turn sickly green unless well watered. Leaves are said to be attractive to deer. Zones 3–9.

Similar: *H. plantaginea* 'Grandiflora', *H.* 'Royal Standard'.

Hosta 'Independence'

Medium, marginally variegated leaves.

Clump size & habit: 30 in. wide × 20 in. high (75 × 50 cm). A shapely, upright mound.

Description: Leaf blade 6½ × 4 in. (16 × 10 cm), of thick substance, satiny very dark green, widely and irregularly margined pale yellow to ivory flecked green, dimpled towards the pointed tip, nearly flat, edge shallowly undulate at its widest part, broadly oval with rounded lobes. Petiole flattish, dark green, finely outlined in ivory white. Flower pale lavender in a dense raceme on an upright, leafy, green, 32 in. (80 cm) scape in high summer; slight fertility.

Comments: Morning sun followed by light shade. Moderate growth rate. Pest resistant. Copious watering and feeding will help to

Hosta 'Independence'

Hosta 'Inniswood'

Hosta 'Invincible'

achieve the widest margin and accentuate the unusual speckling. Superb in containers.

Similar: *H.* 'Olympic Glacier'.

Hosta 'Inniswood'

Medium to large, medio-variegated leaves.

Clump size & habit: 49 in. wide × 24 in. high (122 × 60 cm). A dense mound.

Description: Leaf blade $8\frac{1}{2}$ × $6\frac{1}{2}$ in. (21 × 16 cm), of thick substance, rich golden yellow, widely and irregularly margined dark green with some chartreuse streaking, matt above and glaucous below, heavily seersuckered, edge widely undulate, shallowly cupped or convex, widely oval to nearly round with heart-shaped pinched to overlapping lobes. Petiole stout, chartreuse, finely outlined in dark green. Flower pale lavender on an upright, bare, glaucous chartreuse, 30 in. (75 cm) scape in midsummer; fertile.

Comments: Light to moderate shade. Slow to increase. Pest resistant. Among the most popular medio-variegated hostas. Leaves unfurl dark green, and the bright, golden yellow central variegation takes some weeks to develop. Divide frequently. Zones 4–8.

Similar: **H.* 'Paradigm', **H.* 'Paul's Glory'.

Hosta 'Invincible'

Medium to large, green leaves.

Clump size & habit: 49 in. wide × 20 in. high (122 × 50 cm). A dense mound.

Description: Leaf blade $8\frac{1}{2}$ × $6\frac{1}{2}$ in. (21 × 16 cm), leathery, glossy olive green, widely veined, edge distinctly rippled, folded, wedge-shaped with a pointed tip and heart-shaped open to folded lobes. Petiole narrowly channeled, green, lightly dotted with red. Flower lightly fragrant, occasionally double, palest lavender, on a leaning, very leafy, pale green, 25 in. (63 cm) scape in late summer; fertile.

Comments: Emerges early. Best in morning sun but tolerates sun all day in cooler climates given plenty of water. Not as pest resistant as its name suggests but nonetheless a superb hosta. Sometimes has multibranched scapes in wet summers. Scapes are stained red where the leafy bracts are attached. Zones 3–9.

Similar: *H.* 'Polished Jade', *H.* 'Rippled Honey', *H.* 'Sweet Bo Peep'.

Hosta 'Jack of Diamonds'

Medium, marginally variegated leaves.

Clump size & habit: 20 in. wide × 16 in. high (50 × 40 cm). A dense mound of overlapping leaves.

Description: Leaf blade 7½ × 6½ in. (19 × 16 cm), very thick, leathery, rich blue-green, very widely and irregularly margined yellow turning cream with paler streaking, matt above and glaucous below, seersuckered, edge slightly undulate, shallowly cupped or convex, widely oval with heart-shaped folded lobes. Petiole light green, outlined in cream. Flower near-white in a dense raceme on an upright, leafy, glaucous gray, 16–17 in. (40–43 cm) scape in early to midsummer; fertile.

Comments: The golden yellow margin does not scorch, but site the plant in high, filtered shade for best leaf color. Slow to establish. Pest resistant.

Similar: *H.* 'Cartwheels', *H.* 'Fleeta Brownell Woodroffe', *H.* 'Kara', *H.* 'Merry Sunshine', *H.* 'Wagon Wheels'.

Hosta 'Jack of Diamonds'

Hosta 'Jade Cascade'

Giant, green leaves.

Clump size & habit: 60 in. wide × 40 in. high (150 × 100 cm). A dramatically arching, open mound.

Description: Leaf blade 21 × 8½ in. (53 × 21 cm), of good substance, glossy, bright olive green, slightly dimpled between the conspicuous veins, edge widely rippled, elongated lanceolate to oval with an acute tip and heart-shaped pinched lobes. Petiole deeply channeled, green, up to 15 in. (38 cm) long. Flower pale lavender on a leaning, leafy, green, 42 in. (105 cm) scape, mahogany tinted below the bracts, from mid to late summer; fertility unknown.

Comments: Light to moderate shade. Ideal in woodland. Slow growing. Individual flowers are widely spaced. Zones 3–9.

Similar: *H.* 'Devon Discovery'.

Hosta 'Jade Cascade'

Hosta 'Jimmy Crack Corn'

Large, yellowish leaves.

Clump size & habit: 44 in. wide × 24 in. high (110 × 60 cm). An upright, open mound of horizontal leaves.

Hosta 'Jimmy Crack Corn'

Description: Leaf blade 8½ × 5 in. (21 × 13 cm), of good substance, chartreuse to bright golden yellow, satiny above and thinly glaucous below, veins conspicuously furrowed, dimpled when mature, edges heavily rippled, slightly folded and arching, oval with a recurved tip and heart-shaped pinched lobes. Petiole chartreuse. Flower near-white in dense clusters on an upright, leafy, chartreuse, 24–30 in. (60–75 cm) scape in early summer; fertile.

Comments: Lutescent. Good light or dappled shade in the morning, full shade in the afternoon. The gracefully rippled edge is unusual on a hosta with golden yellow leaves of this size.

Similar: *H.* 'Choo Choo Train', *H.* 'Golden Gate', *H.* 'Sea Gulf Stream'.

Sports: **H.* 'Cornbelt'.

Hosta 'Joseph'

Medium, green leaves.

Clump size & habit: 30 in. wide × 16 in. high (75 × 40 cm). An arching mound.

Hosta 'Joseph' sporting to *H.* 'Queen Josephine'

Description: Leaf blade 6½ × 5½ in. (16 × 14 cm), of thick substance, glossy, dark olive green, veins ribbed, some seersuckering, edge slightly rippled, convex, widely oval to nearly round with heart-shaped open lobes. Petiole narrowly channeled, light olive green, with maroon dots on the reverse. Flower lavender on an upright, leafy, maroon-dotted, 16¾ in. (42 cm) scape in late summer; fertility unknown.

Comments: Light to moderate shade. Differs from its parent *H.* 'Queen Josephine' in having a slower growth rate.

Similar: *H.* 'Black Hills', *H.* 'Lakeside Accolade', **H.* 'Lakeside Black Satin', *H.* 'Second Wind', *H.* 'Spinach Patch', **H. ventricosa*.

Hosta 'June'

Medium, medio-variegated leaves.

Clump size & habit: 30 in. wide × 15 in. high (75 × 38 cm). A symmetrical mound of overlapping leaves.

Description: Leaf blade 6½ × 4 in. (16 × 10 cm), of good substance, smooth, chartreuse turning yellow, finally ivory, irregularly margined blue with pale blue-green streaking, matt above and glaucous below, edge almost flat, slightly cupped, oval with a graceful tip and heart-shaped pinched lobes. Petiole chartreuse-yellow, outlined in blue-green. Flower bell-shaped, near-white, in a dense raceme on a thick, upright, bare, mauve-gray, 22 in. (55 cm) scape in midsummer; fertile.

Comments: For subtle chartreuse and blue tints, grow in light shade in a cool climate; for a harsher contrast expose to morning sunlight. Plants grown in good light are very different from those grown in shade. Moderate to fast growth rate. Easy to cultivate. A superb foreground specimen. Lovely in a shiny blue ceramic pot. Winner of the 2000 Alex J. Summers Distinguished Merit Hosta Award. Named Hosta of the Year by the American Hosta Growers Association in 2001. Divide frequently.

Hosta 'June', a young plant.

Hosta 'June Moon', juvenile leaves.

Hosta 'Key Lime Pie'

Similar: *H.* 'Katherine Lewis', **H.* 'Paradise Joyce', *H.* 'Punky'.

Sports: *H.* 'June Fever' (leaves a shiny, brassy yellow with a narrow, dark green margin), *H.* 'Early Times', **H.* 'English Sunrise' and *H.* 'May' (leaves entirely bright golden yellow), **H.* 'High Society', *H.* 'Touch of Class'.

Hosta 'June Moon'

Medium, marginally variegated leaves.

Clump size & habit: 25 in. wide × 18 in. high (63 × 45 cm). An upright mound.

Description: Leaf blade 9½ × 8½ in. (24 × 21 cm), of thick substance, acid lime-green to chartreuse-yellow, very widely margined ivory to white with some streaking, intensely seersuck-ered and puckered when mature, edge slightly rippled when young, widely oval to nearly round with heart-shaped overlapping lobes. Petiole light green, outlined in ivory. Flower near-white on an upright, bare, glaucous green, 18¾ in. (47 cm) scape in late summer; sterile.

Comments: Morning sun for best leaf base color. Slow to moderate growth rate. Worth every effort to keep the leaves in pristine condition. Puckering over seersuckering on the leaf surface almost amounts to distortion though this is not apparent in juvenile plants.

Similar: **H.* 'Electrum Stater', *H.* 'Joshua's Banner' (leaves smoother).

Hosta 'Key Lime Pie'

Large, marginally variegated leaves.

Clump size & habit: 61 in. wide × 23 in. high (152 × 58 cm). A dense mound.

Description: Leaf blade 11½ × 9 in. (29 × 23 cm), of good substance, rich midgreen, very widely and irregularly margined chartreuse turning ivory with lighter green streaking, matt above and glaucous below, moderately seersuckered, prominently veined, edge attractively rippled, convex, broadly oval with a long, pointed tip and heart-shaped pinched to folded lobes. Petiole stout, light green, finely outlined in ivory. Flower bell-shaped, purple-striped lavender, opening from a rich purple bud, on an arching or leaning, leafy, olive green, 22 in. (55 cm) scape in high summer; fertility unknown.

Comments: Ideal for warmer climates, enjoying morning sun in cooler regions if given plenty of water. Vigorous, fast growing. The central leaf color changes from green to chartreuse-yellow during the season. The flowering portion of the scape is purple tinted. Divide regularly.

Similar: **H.* 'American Icon'.

Hosta 'King Tut'

Medium, yellowish leaves.

Clump size & habit: 30 in. wide × 18¾ in. high (75 × 47 cm). A symmetrical mound.

Description: Leaf blade 8 × 6½ in. (20 × 16 cm), of thick substance, unfurls chartreuse slowly turning yellow, matt above and glaucous below, seersuckered, cupped, widely oval with a small, vestigial tip and heart-shaped open to pinched lobes. Petiole chartreuse. Flower lavender-striped near-white on an upright, leafy, chartreuse, 34¾ in. (87 cm) scape in midsummer; fertile.

Comments: Lutescent. Some morning sun in cooler climates, light shade elsewhere. Among the best medium-sized hostas with golden yellow leaves. Slow to establish. Pest resistant. Has tall flower scapes.

Similar: *H.* 'Golden Medallion', *H.* 'Golden Nugget', *H.* 'Golden Waffles', *H.* 'Treasure'.

Sports: *H.* 'Mister Watson', *H.* 'Tut Tut'.

Hosta 'King Tut'

Hosta 'Kiwi Blue Baby'

Small, very blue leaves.

Clump size & habit: 19 in. wide × 8 in. high (48 × 20 cm). A rounded, symmetrical mound.

Description: Leaf blade 4 × 3 in. (10 × 8 cm), of thick substance, frosty to dark blue, prominently veined, edge nearly flat, flat to convex, widely oval with a long thin tip and heart-shaped pinched to overlapping lobes. Petiole blue-green. Flower bell-shaped, palest lavender, on an upright, bare, blue-green, 10 in. (25 cm) scape in midsummer; sterile.

Comments: Good light or dappled to medium shade. Slow growing. Pest resistant.

Hosta 'Kiwi Blue Baby'

Hosta 'Kiwi Full Monty'

Medium, medio-variegated leaves.

Clump size & habit: 36 in. wide × 18 in. high (90 × 45 cm). An open mound.

Description: Leaf blade 6½ × 3½ in. (16 × 9 cm), of good substance, glaucous, chartreuse turning creamy yellow to ivory, widely margined rich blue-green with occasional silver flecks at the junction between the center and the margin, slight dimpling, edge almost flat, folded, oval with a long thin tip and tapered, open to pinched lobes. Petiole narrowly channeled, chartreuse, outlined in dark blue-green. Flower pinkish lavender, opening from a rich violet bud, in a dense raceme on an upright, leafy, glaucous green, 28 in. (70 cm) scape, purple-tinted toward the raceme, in high summer; poor fertility.

Hosta 'Kiwi Full Monty'

Comments: Good light to light shade to maintain the rich but subtle changing leaf color. Vigorous, fast growing. The large bracts and the flower buds also have silver-white flashes. An outstanding hosta. Divide frequently.

Similar: '*H.* 'Gypsy Rose', **H.* 'Striptease'.

Hosta 'Komodo Dragon'

Giant, green leaves.

Clump size & habit: 73 in. wide × 28 in. high (183 × 70 cm). An open, almost vase-shaped mound.

Description: Leaf blade 15 × 11 in. (38 × 28 cm), thick, blue-tinted dark green, matt above and glaucous below, veins distinct and widely spaced, dimpled, edge conspicuously and evenly rippled, widely oval with a long, thin tip on mature leaves, lobes heart-shaped and open. Petiole stout, blue-green. Flower palest lavender on an upright, leafy, light green, 36 in. (90 cm) scape in midsummer; fertility unknown.

Comments: Light to moderate shade. Rapid growth rate. Pest resistant. An impressive specimen for woodland. The regular, shallow piecrust edge on the leaf is particularly attractive.

Similar: *H.* 'Big Sam', *H.* 'Green Ripples', *H.* 'Lakeside Ripples'.

Hosta 'Krossa Regal'

Large to giant, blue-gray leaves.

Clump size & habit: 71 in. wide × 33 in. high (178 × 83 cm). An upright, arching mound.

Description: Leaf blade 11 × 7 in. (28 × 18 cm), of good substance, smooth, soft gray-blue, widely veined, edge slightly undulate, slightly arching, oval with a long thin tip and rounded, open lobes. Petiole upright, gray-green. Flower lavender on an upright, bare, light gray-green, 60 in. (150 cm) scape in mid to high summer; sterile.

Comments: Dappled to light shade. Pest resistant. Becomes more spreading with maturity. Has great architectural merit as a specimen. Good in large containers if kept well-watered. Outstanding in leaf and flower. Winner of the 2001 Alex J. Summers Distinguished Merit Hosta Award.

Hosta 'Komodo Dragon', a young plant.

Similar: *H. 'Pewter Frost', H. 'Phoenix', *H. 'Snowden', H. 'Tenryu'.

Sports: *H. 'Regal Splendor', H. 'Regalia', H. 'Tom Schmid' (leaves blue-gray with a narrow cream to white margin)

Hosta 'Krugerrand'
Giant, yellow leaves.

Clump size & habit: 72 in. wide × 30 in. high (180 × 75 cm). An impressive upright mound.

Description: Leaf blade 14 × 10 in. (35 × 25 cm), of thick substance, matt chartreuse becoming bright yellow, widely veined, dimpled when mature, edge slightly undulate, convex, nearly round with heart-shaped lobes. Petiole stout, semi-erect, olive green. Flower lavender on an upright to leaning, leafy, olive green, 40 in. (100 cm) scape in midsummer; fertile.

Comments: Lutescent. Dappled to light shade. Moderately slow to increase. Pest resistant. Lovely backed with dark green ferns. The leaves hold their color even in shade.

Similar: *H. 'Zounds'.

Hosta 'Lady Guinevere'
Medium, medio-variegated leaves.

Clump size & habit: 18 in. wide × 10 in. high (45 × 25 cm). A graceful and colorful mound.

Description: Leaf blade 8 × 4 in. (20 × 10 cm), of average substance, chartreuse becoming golden yellow, narrowly and irregularly margined midgreen with paler streaks, matt above and glaucous below, dimpled, widely veined, edge evenly piecrusted, flat, oval with heart-shaped pinched lobes. Petiole chartreuse to yellow, outlined in green. Flower light violet with purple anthers on a leaning to upright, leafy, chartreuse, 27 in. (68 cm) scape in high summer; fertility unknown.

Comments: Best in a lightly shaded border with yellow-leaved hostas and dark green ferns. Good in containers. The variegation is slow to appear. Slow to average growth rate. Avoid pest damage. It is still rare to see medio-variegated hostas with noticeably rippled margins. Divide regularly.

Hosta 'Krossa Regal'

Hosta 'Krugerrand', a young plant.

Hosta 'Lady Guinevere'

Hosta 'Lady Isobel Barnett'

Hosta 'Lakeside Black Satin'

Hosta 'Lady Isobel Barnett'

Large to giant, marginally variegated leaves.

Clump size & habit: 61 in. wide × 30 in. high (152 × 75 cm). A dense mound.

Description: Leaf blade 18 × 10 in. (45 × 25 cm), of thick substance, light olive green, irregularly margined yellow turning cream, satiny above and glaucous below, edge slightly undulate, widely oval to nearly round with a conspicuous tip and heart-shaped overlapping lobes. Petiole leaning, stout, light green, outlined in cream. Flower pale lavender on a pendant, chartreuse, leafy, 44 in. (110 cm) scape in late summer; fertile.

Comments: Grows well in sun or shade given adequate moisture. Moderate to good growth rate. Pest resistant. Lovely with orange daylilies or impressive in a huge container.

Similar: *H.* 'Beauty Substance', *H.* 'Bottom Line', *H.* 'David A. Haskell', *H.* 'Small Sum', *H.* 'Something Good', *H.* 'Sum It Up', *H.* 'Sum of All', *H.* 'Sum Total', *H.* 'Titanic', *H.* 'Vim and Vigor'.

Hosta 'Lakeside Black Satin'

Medium, green leaves.

Clump size & habit: 41 in. wide × 18 in. high (102 × 45 cm). An open mound.

Description: Leaf blade 9 × 8½ in. (23 × 21 cm), of thin substance, lustrous black-green, very glossy below, smooth, widely veined, edge closely and evenly rippled, widely oval with a prominent tip and heart-shaped open lobes. Petiole dark green. Flower widely spaced, bell-shaped, white-striped deep purple, on an upright, bare, dark green, 34¾ in. (87 cm) scape in mid to late summer; fertility unknown.

Comments: Full shade all day. Guard against pest damage. Exceptionally dark green with very widely spaced veins.

Similar: *H.* 'Holly's Honey', *H.* 'Lakeside Coal Miner', **H. ventricosa.*

Hosta 'Lakeside Cha Cha'
Medium, marginally variegated leaves.

Clump size & habit: 27 in. wide × 14 in. high (68 × 35 cm). A semi-upright, open, tiered mound.

Description: Leaf blade 8½ × 6½ in. (21 × 16 cm), of thick substance, soft golden chartreuse, widely and irregularly margined creamy white, satiny above and glaucous below, dimpled, widely veined, edge slightly rippled, mod-erately undulate, widely oval with heart-shaped pinched lobes. Petiole stout, chartreuse, outlined in cream. Flower pale lavender on an upright, leafy, light green, 28 in. (70 cm) scape in mid to late summer; sterile.

Comments: Lutescent. Morning sun in cooler regions, elsewhere light shade all day. Leaves gradually assume a bright yellow glow.

Similar: *H.* 'Saint Elmo's Fire' (habit not very vigorous).

Hosta 'Lakeside Dragonfly'
Small to medium, marginally variegated leaves.

Clump size & habit: 30 in. wide × 18 in. high (75 × 45 cm). An arching mound.

Description: Leaf blade 7 × 3½ in. (18 × 9 cm), of thin substance, midblue-green, widely margined chartreuse turning white, with gray-green streaking, satiny above and matt below, edge shallowly undulate, broadly lanceolate with an acute tip and tapered lobes. Petiole narrowly

Hosta 'Lakeside Cha Cha'

Hosta 'Lakeside Dragonfly'

channeled, blue-green, outlined in white. Flower 2 in. (5 cm) long, pale lavender, on an upright, bare, blue-influenced green 30 in. (75 cm) scape from high to late summer; fertile.

Comments: Needs light shade to keep its blue leaf color. Good in a container or towards the front of the border with astilbes, dicentras, and liriopes. Forms a very tight mature clump. The thinness of the leaves can cause some leaf blade edges to roll inwards giving a canoelike effect.

Similar: *H.* 'Soft Shoulders'.

Hosta 'Lakeside Kaleidoscope'

Small, marginally variegated leaves.

Clump size & habit: 15 in. wide × 8½ in. high (38 × 21 cm). A compact mound.

Description: Leaf blade 6½ × 4 in. (16 × 10 cm), of thick substance, shiny, blue-green, widely and irregularly margined creamy white with many gray-green streaks, strongly veined, edge variably undulate, widely oval with a distinct tip and with heart-shaped pinched lobes. Petiole blue-green, outlined in creamy white.

Hosta 'Lakeside Kaleidoscope'

Flower near-white on an upright, leafy, green-streaked, 24 in. (60 cm) scape in late summer; fertile.

Comments: Easy to grow. Best in shade all day. Vigorous, fast growing. Leaves markedly widen with maturity. An extremely attractive small hosta with striking color combinations. Very wide-feathered margin; sometimes more than half the leaf is variegated.

Hosta 'Lakeside Love Affaire'

Hosta 'Lakeside Lollipop'

Small, green leaves.

Clump size & habit: 16 in. wide × 8½ in. high (40 × 21 cm). A low, spreading mound.

Description: Leaf blade 3½ × 3 in. (9 × 8 cm), of thick substance, shiny dark green, seersuckered, veins prominent, edge flat, nearly round with rounded, open lobes. Petiole lighter green, appearing to pierce the blade. Flower pure white on an upright, leafy, dark green, 16 in. (40 cm) scape in midsummer; fertile.

Comments: Light to moderate shade. Slow to increase. Use in the foreground. Ideal for a gravel garden. The almost round leaf blade and petiole form the shape of a lollipop.

Hosta 'Lakeside Lollipop'

Hosta 'Lakeside Love Affaire'

Large, medio-variegated leaves.

Clump size & habit: 36 in. wide × 18 in. high (90 × 45 cm). An upright, flaring mound.

Description: Leaf blade 9 × 7 in. (23 × 18 cm), of thick substance, white, widely margined dark green with chartreuse streaking, satiny above and matt below, veins prominent and widely spaced, edge slightly rippled, widely oval with heart-shaped open to pinched lobes. Petiole white, sharply outlined in dark green. Flower near-white on an upright, bare, 22 in. (55 cm) light green scape from mid to late summer; fertile.

Comments: Light to moderate shade all day. Moderate growth rate. Lovely with the gray-leaved fern *Otophorum okonum* or *Athyrium*

Hosta 'Lakeside Shore Master'

Hosta 'Lakeside Zinger'

Hosta 'Lancifolia'

'Ghost'. Has great sculptural qualities as well as striking tricolor leaves. Divide frequently.

Hosta 'Lakeside Shore Master'
Medium, medio-variegated leaves.

Clump size & habit: 30 in. wide × 14 in. high (75 × 35 cm). An open mound.

Description: Leaf blade 10 × 8½ in. (25 × 21 cm), of thick substance, ivory rapidly turning light green to rich yellow, very widely and irregularly margined dark blue-green with light blue-green streaking, matt above and satiny below, intensely seersuckered, edge flat, slightly cupped, oval with pinched to overlapping lobes. Petiole chartreuse-yellow, outlined in dark green. Flower pale lavender on an upright, leafy, chartreuse, 18–22 in. (45–55 cm) scape in high summer; fertile.

Comments: Good light to moderate shade. Rapid growth rate. Pest resistant. A very colorful hosta with a pleasing leaf habit. Divide frequently.

Hosta 'Lakeside Zinger'
Small, marginally variegated leaves.

Clump size & habit: 9 in. wide × 6½ in. high (23 × 16 cm). A low, dense mound.

Description: Leaf blade 3 × 1½ in. (8 × 4 cm), thin, smooth, satiny olive green, irregularly margined pure white with streaks jetting toward the midrib, edge randomly undulate, oval with rounded, open lobes. Petiole shallowly channeled, green, clearly outlined in white. Flower pale lavender on an upright, dark, leafy, green, 11–18 in. (28–45 cm) scape in mid to high summer; fertile.

Comments: Good light to moderate shade. Rapid growth rate, quickly forming a clump. Green dotting on the leaf margin. Large conspicuous variegated flower bracts.

Hosta 'Lancifolia'
Small to medium, green leaves.

Clump size & habit: 41 in. wide × 16 in. high (102 × 40 cm). A dense, spreading mound.

Description: Leaf blade 7 × 2½ in. (18 × 6 cm), of thin substance, mid to dark green, shiny above and glossy below, edge slightly undulate, elliptic to narrowly oval with an acute tip and tapered, open to pinched lobes. Petiole green, purple-dotted toward the crown. Flower narrowly bell-shaped, lavender, in a dense raceme on an upright, leafy, purple-dotted, green, 20 in. (50 cm) scape in late summer; limited fertility.

Comments: Emerges early; leaves may be damaged by spring frost. Light shade. Vigorous and floriferous. Excellent beginner's hosta. Lovely in a large wooden container. Zones 3–9.

Similar: *H. cathayana.*

Sports: *H.* 'Lancifolia Aurea' (leaves chartreuse-yellow).

Hosta 'Leading Lady'
Large, marginally variegated leaves.

Clump size & habit: 41 in. wide × 22 in. high (102 × 55 cm). An upright, moderately dense mound.

Description: Leaf blade 14 × 10 in. (35 × 25 cm), of thick substance, dark olive green, narrowly and irregularly margined rich golden yellow turning creamy white with chartreuse streaking, satiny above and glaucous below, prominently veined, dimpled and puckered, edge widely undulate, convex toward the distinct tip, widely oval with heart-shaped pinched to overlapping lobes. Petiole narrowly channeled, pale green, finely outlined in cream.

Hosta 'Leading Lady'

Flower pale lavender on an upright, leafy, glaucous green, 38¾ in. (97 cm) scape in late summer; fertility unknown.

Comments: Light to full shade. Moderate growth rate. A superb specimen hosta. Mature plants show a paler green band of feathering between the margin and the base color of the leaf.

Similar: **H.* 'Sagae'.

Hosta 'Lederhosen'

Medium, blue-green leaves.

Clump size & habit: 24 × 12 in. (60 × 30 cm). A flattish mound of almost horizontal leaves.

Description: Leaf blade 7½ × 5 in. (19 × 13 cm), of thick substance, matt to shiny, rich blue-green, smooth, widely veined, edge deeply undulate, oval with a recurved tip and open lobes. Petiole near horizontal, blue-green. Flower fragrant, white, opening from a very pale lavender bud, on an upright, leafy, green, 15 in. (38 cm) scape in late summer; fertility unknown.

Comments: Needs shade in the warmest climates or some morning sun in coolest areas to promote maximum growth. Leaves turn midgreen in bright light. Vigorous. The tough, leathery leaves have a fancied resemblance to the German britches known as "lederhosen."

Similar: *H.* 'Bob Deane'.

Hosta 'Lemon Lime'

Miniature, yellowish leaves.

Clump size & habit: 36 in. wide × 12 in. high (90 × 30 cm). A tight, dense mound.

Description: Leaf blade 3½ × 1¼ in. (9 × 3 cm), of thin substance, chartreuse, turning yellow toward the edges, matt above and glossy whitish green below, prominently veined, edge rippled, folded, widely lanceolate with rounded to tapered, open lobes. Petiole narrowly channeled, green. Flower deep purple-striped rich violet, opening from a green bud, on an upright, bare, green, 12–18 in. (30–45 cm) scape from midsummer; fertile.

Comments: May produce three flushes of leaves each season. Some rebloom in late summer if the first scapes are removed after flowering. Leaves remain chartreuse unless in bright light. Not sun tolerant. Vigorous, fast growing.

Hosta 'Lederhosen'

Makes carpets of pointed leaves above which rise tall scapes. Zones 3–9.

Similar: *H.* 'Chartreuse Waves', *H.* 'Feather Boa', *H.* 'Hydon Sunset', *H.* 'Ogon Koba'.

Sports: *H.* 'Iced Lemon', *H.* 'Lemon Delight', *H.* 'Lemon Frost' (as vigorous as its parent) and *H.* 'Lemon Sorbet' (leaves greenish yellow with a pure white margin), *H.* 'Lime Meringue' (leaves midgreen with a white margin), *H.* 'Twist of Lime'.

Hosta 'Liberty'

Large to giant, marginally variegated leaves.

Clump size & habit: 38¾ in. wide × 28 in. high (97 × 70 cm). An upright mound.

Description: Leaf blade: 12½ in. × 9 in. (31 × 23 cm), of good substance, dark blue-green turning green, widely margined golden yellow turning ivory-cream jetting toward the midrib, matt to glaucous above and glaucous below, edge flat, folded, widely oval with a vestigial tip and heart-shaped open to overlapping lobes. Petiole narrowly channeled, green, outlined in cream. Flower lavender in profusion on a thick, leaning, leafy, intensely glaucous, 49 in. (122 cm) scape in high to late summer; fertile.

Comments: Light to moderate shade. Use as a specimen in the border, with plenty of moisture available to encourage the leaf to widen. The 2½ in. (6 cm) wide margin is spectacular.

Similar: *H.* 'Clifford's Forest Fire', *H.* 'Ivory Coast' (leaf edge rippled), **H.* 'Magic Fire'.

Hosta 'Lemon Lime'

Hosta 'Liberty'

Hosta 'Little Black Scape'

Hosta 'Little Caesar'

Hosta 'Little Black Scape'

Medium, yellowish leaves.

Clump size & habit: 24 in. wide × 10 in. high (60 × 25 cm). A compact mound.

Description: Leaf blade 5 × 4½ in. (13 × 11 cm), of good substance, matt chartreuse-green turning golden yellow, dimpled, widely veined, edge mainly flat but kinked toward the base, oval with an acute tip and tapered, open lobes. Petiole short, light green. Flower lavender, opening from a violet bud, on an upright or leaning, occasionally leafy, glossy, darkest purple to black, 22 in. (55 cm) scape in midsummer; not fertile in warmer climates, unknown elsewhere.

Comments: Lutescent. Morning sun enhances leaf and scape colors. Moderate growth rate. Plant with *Hemerocallis* 'Sir Blackstem' and *Ophiopogon planiscapus* 'Nigrescens' to create an eye-catching effect. The dusky scapes and violet flower buds among the chartreuse-yellow foliage make this one of the most distinct and unusual hostas.

Hosta 'Little Caesar'

Miniature, medio-variegated leaves.

Clump size & habit: 12 in. wide × 5 in. high (30 × 13 cm). An upright mound.

Description: Leaf blade 3 × 1½ in. (8 × 4 cm), of good substance, smooth, ivory white, irregularly margined midgreen, satiny above and glossy below, edge slightly rippled, undulate to twisted, folded, lanceolate with a conspicuous tip and wedge-shaped to tapered, open lobes. Petiole ivory, outlined in green. Flower violet-striped lavender on an upright, leafy, light green, 8½–10 in. (21–25 cm) scape in mid to high summer; fertility unknown.

Comments: Among the best of the smaller white-centered, green-margined hostas. Unusually good substance. Rapid growth rate. Divide frequently. Leaves more pronouncedly twisted when young.

Similar: *H.* 'Medusa', *H.* 'Mountain Fog', *H.* 'Surprised by Joy'.

Hosta 'Little Sunspot'

Small, medio-variegated leaves.

Clump size & habit: 30 in. wide × 10 in. high (75 × 25 cm). A compact mound.

Description: Leaf blade 5 × 4 in. (13 × 10 cm), of thick substance, rich yellow, widely margined vivid dark green with subtle dark to light chartreuse streaks, matt above and satiny below, seersuckered, edge slightly rippled, slightly cupped, widely oval to nearly round with heart-shaped pinched lobes. Petiole chartreuse, outlined in green. Flower pale lavender to near-white on an upright to leaning, olive green, 10–18 in. (25–45 cm) scape in midsummer; fertile.

Comments: Needs morning sun in cooler regions for the leaf center to turn brilliant gold, elsewhere site in shade all day. Outstanding in leaf form and color contrast. Divide frequently.

Similar: *H.* 'Amy Elizabeth', *H.* 'Just So', *H.* 'Not So'.

Hosta 'Lonesome Dove'

Medium, medio-variegated leaves.

Clump size & habit: 32½ in. wide × 17 in. high (81 × 43 cm). An upright mound.

Hosta 'Little Sunspot'

Hosta 'Lonesome Dove'

Description: Leaf blade 6 × 4¾ in. (15 × 12 cm), of heavy substance, ivory white, very widely and irregularly margined glaucous blue-green with gray-green streaking, seersuckered, edge flat, cupped, rounded with a pointed tip and heart-shaped pinched to folded lobes. Petiole leaning, ivory, outlined in blue-green. Flower pale lavender on an upright, bare, blue-green, 18 in. (45 cm) scape from mid to high summer; fertility unknown.

Comments: Best in cooler gardens in shade or lowish light as heat turns the bluish margins shiny green. Site away from trees as falling debris damages the leaves. Lovely with ferns and other lacy foliage. The flower has a darker lavender pattern on the petal center. Divide frequently.

Similar: *H.* 'Lakeside Beach Captain', *H.* 'Lakeside Cup Cake', *H.* 'Summer Joy'.

Hosta longissima

Small, green leaves.

Clump size & habit: 25 in. wide × 9½ in. high (63 × 24 cm). A low, arching, dense mound.

Description: Leaf blade 8 × 1 in. (20 × 2.5 cm), of average substance, midgreen, matt above and shiny below, smooth, edge flat with an occasional kink, linear to lanceolate with an acute tip, graduating into the purple-dotted petiole. Flower purple on an upright, leafy, light green, 22 in. (55 cm) scape from early to late autumn; fertile.

Comments: Shade all day and abundant moisture. Can be grown in garden ponds successfully if the crown is kept above the water line. The strap-shaped leaves are among the narrowest in the genus.

Similar: *H.* 'Bitsy Green', *H. longissima* 'Brevifolia'.

Hosta 'Love Pat'

Medium to large, very blue leaves.

Clump size & habit: 40 in. wide × 20 in. high (100 × 50 cm). A dense mound.

Description: Leaf blade 8½ × 8 in. (21 × 20 cm), of thick substance, rich blue, intensely seersuckered, deeply cupped, nearly round with a vestigial tip and heart-shaped overlapping lobes. Petiole stout, blue-green. Flower near bell-shaped, palest lavender to near-white, in a dense raceme on a leafy, grayish mauve, 22¾ in. (57 cm) scape, barely rising above the leaf mound, in midsummer; fertile.

Comments: Good light to light shade all day. Avoid planting under trees where the leaves will collect falling debris. In the hottest climates it turns dark green after midsummer. Slow to increase when young, faster when mature. Pest resistant. Leaves upwardly poised and very cupped so that the glaucous undersides are often visible. Zones 3–7.

Similar: *H.* 'Blue Rock', *H.* 'Blue Splendor', *H.* 'Rock and Roll'.

Hosta longissima

Hosta 'Magic Fire'

Large, marginally variegated leaves.

Clump size & habit: 30 in. wide × 20 in. high (75 × 50 cm). A spectacular upright mound.

Description: Leaf blade 10 × 7½ in. (25 × 19 cm), of thick substance, matt midgreen, very widely margined yellow turning ivory with gray-green streaking, widely veined, edge flat, undulate, broadly oval with a vestigial tip and heart-shaped folded lobes. Petiole stout, green, outlined in ivory. Flower lavender on an upright, leafy, purple-tinted green, 36 in. (90 cm) scape in high summer; fertile.

Comments: Light shade. Site amid darker green, plainer foliage to contrast with its show-stopping, flamelike variegation. Slow to establish. Pest resistant. The twisted and dramatically variegated leaves give great garden presence.

Similar: *H.* 'Clifford's Forest Fire', **H.* 'Liberty'.

Hosta 'Love Pat'

Hosta
'Magic Fire'

Hosta 'Mardi Gras'

Large, marginally variegated leaves.

Clump size & habit: 60 in. wide × 28 in. (150 × 70 cm). A widely spreading clump.

Description: Leaf blade 14 × 11 in. (35 × 28 cm), of thick substance, mid to dark green, irregularly margined ivory with lighter green streaking, glossy above and matt below, prominently veined, edge randomly kinked, broadly oval with a pointed tip and heart-shaped folded to pinched lobes. Petiole green, outlined in ivory. Flower palest lavender to almost white on an upright, leafy, light green, 36 in. (90 cm) scape in early summer; fertile.

Comments: Light to moderate shade. A superb background hosta. Slow to establish but ul-

Hosta 'Mardi Gras'

Hosta 'Marilyn'

timately very large. Pest resistant. Grow with *H.* 'Daybreak' to light up a dark corner. The leaves retain their blue overlay in low light.

Similar: *H.* 'Mike Shadrack'.

Hosta 'Marilyn'

Small to medium, yellowish leaves.

Clump size & habit: 30 in. wide × 12 in. high (75 × 30 cm). A dense mound.

Description: Leaf blade 8½ × 3½ in. (21 × 9 cm), of average to good substance, chartreuse soon turning golden yellow becoming bright gold by high summer, veins distinctly ribbed, slight dimpling, edge widely undulate and rolled under, heart-shaped with an occasionally recurved tip and with tapered, open to pinched lobes. Petiole chartreuse to yellow. Flower pale lavender on an upright, bare, chartreuse, 24 in. (60 cm) scape in high summer; fertility unknown.

Comments: Lutescent. Easily exceeds its registered dimensions. Leaves emerge early needing protection from late frosts in cooler climates; elsewhere morning sun enhances the leaf color. A hosta with nice movement to its leaves.

Hosta 'Marilyn Monroe'

Medium, green leaves.

Clump size & habit: 24 in. wide × 12 in. high (60 × 30 cm). An upright mound of piecrust-edged leaves.

Description: Leaf blade 7 × 5 in. (18 × 13 cm), of thick substance, grayish green, matt above and glaucous white below, widely veined, smooth, edge evenly rippled, oval to nearly round with a distinct tip and heart-shaped pinched to folded lobes. Petiole pale green, with red dots. Flower purple-striped pale lavender on an upright, leafy, purple-dotted pale green, 18 in. (45 cm) scape in high summer; very fertile.

Comments: Light to moderate shade. Vigorous. Produces exceptional seedlings. The widely ruffled edges recurve, revealing the white undersides. Dark purple anthers contrast with the paler lavender petals.

Similar: *H.* 'Candy Dish' (habit smaller), **H.* 'Harry van der Laar'.

Hosta 'Maui Buttercups'

Small, yellowish leaves.

Clump size & habit: 14 in. wide × 10 in. high (35 × 25 cm). A diffuse, upward-facing mound.

Description: Leaf blade 5 × 4 in. (13 × 10 cm), of thick substance, chartreuse to bright yellow, shiny above and glaucous below, intensely seersuckered and puckered toward the tip, edge flat, deeply cupped to folded, nearly round with heart-shaped pinched to overlapping lobes. Petiole widely channeled, flattish, chartreuse to yellow. Flower green-tipped palest lavender on an upright, sturdy, leafy, glaucous chartreuse, 18 in. (45 cm) scape in late summer; fertile.

Comments: Lutescent. Early morning sun then dappled shade in cooler climates, denser shade in warmer climates. Slow to establish but eventually a moderate growth rate. Very large leafy bracts along the scape and around the raceme. A superb small yellow hosta having great presence.

Similar: H. 'Eye Catcher', *H. 'Golden Teacup', H. 'Little Aurora'.

Sports: H. 'Rainforest Sunrise' (a much-sought after newish hosta with yellow-margined dark green leaves).

Hosta 'Memories of Dorothy'

Medium, variegated leaves.

Clump size & habit: 42¾ in. wide × 18 in. high (107 × 45 cm). A dense mound.

Description: Leaf blade 10-½ × 7 in. (26 × 18 cm), of average substance, midgreen with a blue cast, irregularly margined and streaked chartreuse gradually turning ivory, satiny above and glaucous white below, closely veined, dimpled to seersuckered, broadly oval with a pointed tip and heart-shaped folded or pinched lobes. Petiole reddish. Flower pale lavender-striped white on a leaning, leafy, occasionally branched, 32 in. (80 cm.) scape from high to late summer; fertile.

Comments: Needs light shade to maintain the blueness on the leaves. Moderate growth rate. The seasonal, subtle tonal contrasts make this hosta a worthy contender for a place in every collection.

Hosta 'Marilyn Monroe'

Hosta 'Maui Buttercups'

Hosta 'Memories of Dorothy'

Hosta 'Metallic Sheen'

Hosta 'Metallica'

Hosta 'Metallic Sheen'

Large to giant, blue-gray leaves.

    Clump size & habit: 60 in. wide × 28 in. high (150 × 70 cm). An open mound.

    Description: Leaf blade 14 × 10 in. (35 × 25 cm), very thick, smooth, metallic gray-blue turning dark green, seersuckered and puckered, edge almost flat, shallowly cupped or convex, widely oval to nearly round with heart-shaped open to overlapping lobes. Petiole stout, light blue-gray to green. Flower glaucous pale lavender on an upright or leaning, leafy, 30–40 in. (75–100 cm) scape in late summer; fertile.

    Comments: Morning sun in cooler climates, elsewhere light shade all day. Slow to moderate growth rate. Pest resistant. Inherits its huge leaves from *H.* 'Sum and Substance' and its thick, texture from *H. sieboldiana* 'Elegans'. Makes a bold statement in the garden.

Hosta 'Metallica'

Medium, blue-green leaves.

    Clump size & habit: 21 in. wide × 16 in. high (53 × 40 cm). A dense mound.

    Description: Leaf blade 7½ × 4 in. (19 × 10 cm), of average substance, dark blue-green turning shiny dark green by high summer, slightly dimpled, veins closely ribbed, edge rippled, slightly twisted, folded, widely oval with heart-shaped pinched to overlapping lobes. Petiole

Hosta 'Midas Touch'

light blue-green. Flower rich lavender on an upright, leafy, blue-green, 25–30 in. (63–75 cm) scape in high summer; fertility unknown.

Comments: Light to moderate shade. Slowish. Pest resistant. Easily exceeds its registered dimensions in good growing conditions.

Hosta 'Midas Touch'

Medium, yellowish leaves.

Clump size & habit: 40 in. wide × 20 in. high (100 × 50 cm). A dense mound.

Description: Leaf blade 8¾ × 8 in. (22 × 20 cm), of thick substance, emerging soft pale chartreuse becoming bright yellow, matt above and glaucous below, intensely seersuckered to deeply puckered, edge shallowly undulate, deeply cupped, nearly round with a vestigial tip and heart-shaped pinched lobes. Petiole chartreuse to muted gold. Flower pale lavender-striped near-white, opening from gray buds in a dense raceme on a leafy, upright, pale green, 24 in. (60 cm) scape in early summer; fertility unknown.

Comments: Lutescent. Leaves retain a green undertone in shade but assume a brassy, metallic hue in strong sunlight. Slow to establish. Pest resistant. Distinguished from most other yellow-leaved hostas by the pebbled surface of the leaf and the deep cupping that reveals the leaf underside. Not suitable for containers.

Similar: *H.* 'Aspen Gold', **H.* 'King Tut', *H.* 'Lime Krinkles', *H.* 'Thai Brass'.

Hosta 'Miki'

Large, yellowish leaves.

Clump size & habit: 50½ in. wide × 22 in. high (126 × 55 cm). A dense, somewhat unruly mound.

Description: Leaf blade 11 × 8½ in. (28 × 21 cm), of thick substance, chartreuse turning bright yellow, matt above and shiny below, prominently veined, some dimpling when mature, edge slightly undulate, convex, widely oval with heart-shaped open to pinched lobes. Petiole sturdy, chartreuse-green. Flower lavender on

Hosta 'Miki'

Hosta 'Mildred Seaver'

an upright to semi-erect, leafy, olive green, 36 in. (90 cm) scape in high summer; fertile.

Comments: Lutescent. Needs light shade to retain the brilliant leaf color. Slow to moderate. Good as a specimen, or in woodland where it lights up dark areas. Pest resistant. Some leaves exhibit pleating towards the tip when mature.

Similar: *H.* 'Alice Gladden', *H.* 'Solar Flare'.

Hosta 'Mildred Seaver'

Large, marginally variegated leaves.

Clump size & habit: 51 in. wide × 20 in. high (127 × 50 cm). A dense mound.

Description: Leaf blade 9 × 8½ in. (23 × 21 cm), of thick substance, mid to dark green, widely and irregularly margined bright golden yellow turning ivory white with gray-green splashes, matt above and thinly glaucous below, moderately seersuckered, edge slightly rippled, slightly arching, widely oval with heart-shaped pinched lobes. Petiole dark green, outlined in yellow. Flower pale lavender on an upright, leafy, green, 22½ in. (56 cm) scape in mid to late summer; fertile.

Comments: Light to moderate shade. Moderate to good growth rate. Easily exceeds the registered dimensions in optimum conditions. Good in containers and in borders or woodland.

Similar: *H.* 'Crusader', *H.* 'Fringe Benefit', *H.* 'Goldbrook Gratis', *H.* 'Leola Fraim'.

Hosta 'Millenium'

Giant, blue-green leaves.

Clump size & habit: 54 in. wide × 36 in. high (135 × 90 cm). An upright, open mound.

Description: Leaf blade 16¾ × 14 in. (42 × 35 cm), of thick substance, glaucous intense blue-green turning green, seersuckered, puckered and crimped, prominently veined, edge slightly undulate, shallowly cupped or convex, widely oval to nearly round with heart-shaped pinched to overlapping lobes. Petiole stout, pale green. Flower white on an upright, bare, thick, 43½–50 in. (109–125 cm) scape in high summer; fertile.

Comments: Cool, moist shade all day. Slow to increase. Pest resistant.

Similar: **H.* 'Metallic Sheen'.

Hosta 'Millenium'

Hosta 'Mississippi Delta'

Hosta montana, flowers

Hosta 'Mississippi Delta'

Giant, blue-gray leaves.

Clump size & habit: 57 in. wide × 36 in. high (142 × 90 cm). An open mound of bright, outward-facing leaves.

Description: Leaf blade 12¾ × 12 in. (32 × 30 cm), very thick, rubbery, blue-gray, dimpled and puckered, edge slightly undulate, flat to shallowly cupped, nearly round with heart-shaped pinched to folded lobes. Petiole stout, blue-green. Flower long, near-white, in a dense raceme on an upright or leaning, light blue-green, 40 in. (100 cm) scape in high summer; fertile.

Comments: Leaf surface soon loses its glaucous coating leaving a rubbery effect, so for best color grow this plant in light woodland with azaleas and hydrangeas. Moderate growth rate. Pest resistant. Zones 3–9.

Hosta montana

Large to giant, green leaves.

Clump size & habit: 48½ in. wide × 24 in. high (121 × 60 cm). An upright mound.

Description: Leaf blade 12 × 9 in. (30 × 23 cm), of thick substance, olive green, satiny above, glossy below and rough to the touch, veins deeply furrowed, slightly dimpled when mature, edge shallowly undulate, arching, slightly folded, widely oval with a long thin tip and heart-shaped overlapping lobes. Petiole stout, light green. Flower suffused lavender to almost white in a dense raceme on a leaning, very leafy, 49 in. (122 cm) scape in midsummer; fertile.

Comments: Some morning sun in cooler climates, light to full shade in warmer climates. Usually much larger in cultivation than in the wild. The heavy pod production weighs down the scape.

Similar: *H.* 'Elatior'.

Sports: *H.* 'Choko Nishiki' (syn. *H.* 'On Stage', leaves golden yellow with a green margin and green streaks), **H. montana* 'Aureomarginata' (emerges much earlier), *H. montana* 'Macrophylla' (leaves wider), *H. montana* 'Mountain Snow' (leaves green with a white margin and white streaks).

Hosta montana 'Aureomarginata'

Hosta montana 'Aureomarginata'

Large, marginally variegated leaves.

Clump size & habit: 65 in. wide × 27 in. high (163 × 68 cm). A cascading mound.

Description: Leaf blade 15 × 8½ in. (38 × 21 cm), of average substance, rich dark green, widely and irregularly margined golden yellow to creamy white with chartreuse streaking, matt above and glossy below and rough to the touch, veins closely spaced, edge slightly undulate, arching, oval with a pointed tip and heart-shaped pinched to overlapping lobes. Petiole widely channeled, green, outlined in yellow. Flower pale lavender in a dense raceme on a leaning, leafy, light green, 38½ in. (96 cm) scape in mid to high summer; seedpods numerous; fertile.

Comments: Light to moderate shade. Moderate growth rate. Not easy to grow but among the most eye-catching variegated introductions. Emerges early, so protect vulnerable new shoots from pest damage; late frosts can scorch the leaves. Winner of the 1985 Alex J. Summers Distinguished Merit Hosta Award. Zones 3–9.

Sports: *H.* 'Ebb Tide' (habit smaller), *H.* 'Mountain Haze' (leaves dark green with a creamy white margin).

Hosta 'Mount Tom'

Medium to large, marginally variegated leaves.

Clump size & habit: 36 in. wide × 19 in. high (90 × 48 cm). A well-poised semi-upright mound.

Description: Leaf blade 11 × 10 in. (28 × 25 cm), of thick substance, dark green with a blue cast, very widely and irregularly margined ivory with chartreuse streaks and splashes, matt above and glaucous below, seersuckered, edge

Hosta 'Mount Tom', a young plant

randomly kinked, broadly oval with rounded pinched to folded lobes. Petiole stout, dark green, outlined in ivory. Flower palest lavender to near-white in a dense raceme on an upright, leafy, dark green, 24 in. (60 cm) scape in mid to high summer; fertile.

Comments: Light to moderate shade to preserve the bluish leaf. Slow to increase. Eventually has one of the widest variegated margins of any hosta. Pest resistant.

Hosta 'Mourning Dove'

Medium, marginally variegated leaves.

Clump size & habit: 31½ × wide × 12 in. high (79 × 30 cm). A low, spreading mound.

Description: Leaf blade 8 × 4 in. (20 × 10 cm), of good substance, soft blue-gray, irregularly margined muted lime-green turning creamy yellow with paler streaking, glaucous above, silvery white indumentum below, smooth, edge

Hosta 'Mourning Dove'

flat, arching, lanceolate to oval narrowing to a point, lobes open to pinched. Petiole blue-gray, outlined in cream. Flower pale lavender with darker lavender markings on an arching, bare, blue-gray, 16–20½ in. (40–51 cm) scape in late summer; fertile.

Comments: Low light to moderate shade. Slow to establish. Lovely in a container or grown with ferns and shade-loving yellow grasses such as *Millium effusum* 'Aureum' and *Carex elata* 'Aurea'. Divide frequently.

Hosta 'Niagara Falls'

Large, green leaves.

Clump size & habit: 30 in. wide × 20 in. high (75 × 50 cm). An open, spreading mound.

Description: Leaf blade 15 × 9 in. (38 × 23 cm), of thick substance, dark green, smooth, matt to glaucous above and shiny below, veins deeply impressed, edge with small, even ripples,

arching, widely oblong to oval with heart-shaped pinched lobes. Petiole stout, pale green. Flower palest lavender on a leaning, leafy, 48 in. (120 cm) scape; fertility unknown.

Comments: Light to full shade all day. Dimensions are much larger in optimum growing conditions. Glaucous bloom on the leaf assumes a waxy sheen later. Piecrust edges are not present on young plants.

Similar: *H.* 'Hoosier Dome', *H.* 'Lakeside Ripples'.

Hosta 'Night Before Christmas'

Medium to large, medio-variegated leaves.

Clump size & habit: 30 in. wide × 18 in. high (75 × 45 cm). A moderately dense, semi-upright mound.

Description: Leaf blade 8½ × 3 in. (21 × 8 cm), of average substance, white, widely and irregularly margined dark olive green with

Hosta 'Niagara Falls'

some streaking, satiny above and shiny below, dimpled, widely veined, edge almost flat, undulate to twisting, oval with an elongated tip and heart-shaped open to pinched lobes. Petiole narrow, ivory, finely outlined in dark green. Flower pendant, pale lavender, on an upright, leafy, ivory, 25 in. (63 cm) scape in midsummer; sterile.

Hosta 'Night Before Christmas'

Comments: Early to emerge. Bright light to moderate shade. Differs from its parent *H.* 'White Christmas' in being larger and stronger and in having less leaf variegation. Divide frequently. Use as a midground specimen with blue-leaved hostas.

Similar: *H.* 'Undulata Univittata'.

Hosta nigrescens

Large to giant, blue-green leaves.

Clump size & habit: 62 in. wide × 30 in. high (155 × 75 cm). A semi-upright mound.

Description: Leaf blade 12 × 10 in. (30 × 25 cm), of thick substance, emerging blue-green then turning dark green, intensely glaucous below, seersuckered, edge almost flat, deeply cupped, widely oval to nearly round with heart-shaped pinched lobes. Petiole stout, ash-gray. Flower purple-streaked pale lavender on an upright, glaucous gray, leafy, 44 in. (110 cm) scape in late summer; barely fertile.

Comments: Light to full shade all day. Moderate growth rate. Pest resistant. Grow small hostas and other ground-covering plants at its

Hosta nigrescens

feet. Shoots emerge almost black. Scapes tower above the foliage. Winner of the 1997 Alex J. Summers Distinguished Merit Hosta Award.

Similar: *H.* 'Kelly', *H.* 'Naegato'.

Hosta 'Olive Branch'

Small, medio-variegated leaves.

Clump size & habit: 24 in. wide × 10 in. high (60 × 25 cm). A mound of overlapping leaves.

Description: Leaf blade 3 × 3 in. (8 × 8 cm), of thin substance, smooth, muted butterscotch-yellow, widely margined olive green with chartreuse streaking, satiny above and glaucous below, widely veined, edge rippled, flat, broadly oval with a distinct tip and heart-shaped overlapping lobes. Petiole narrow, chartreuse, finely outlined in olive green. Flower opening from a large ballooning bud, on an upright or leaning, bare, gray-green, 25 in. (63 cm) scape in midsummer; fertile.

Comments: Bright light to moderate shade. Rapid growth rate. Prone to pest damage. Divide frequently.

Hosta 'One Man's Treasure'

Medium, green leaves.

Clump size & habit: 24 in. wide × 14 in. high (60 × 35 cm). An open, arching mound.

Description: Leaf blade 6½ × 5½ in. (16 × 14 cm), of thick substance, leathery, mid to dark green, matt above and glossy below, widely veined, edges undulate, widely oval with an

Hosta 'Olive Branch'

Hosta 'One Man's Treasure'

Hosta 'Opipara Bill Brincka'

Hosta 'Ops'

Hosta 'Osprey'

elegant tip and heart-shaped to flat open lobes. Petiole shallow, olive green, intensely burgundy dotted. Flower bell-shaped, violet, white-striped inside, on a stout, upright, leafy, deep burgundy red, 20–24 in. (50– 60 cm) scape in early autumn; fertile.

Comments: Light to moderate shade. Moderate growth rate. Distinguished by purple-black scapes, purple-stained flower bracts, deep violet pedicels and flower tubes, and mahogany-purple dotting on both sides of the petiole seeping into the leaf blade. Outstanding, particularly when in flower. Plant with *Mitella stylosa*, which also has burgundy leaf stems.

Similar: **H.* 'Cinnamon Sticks', *H.* 'Granddaddy Redlegs', *H.* 'Swizzle Sticks'.

Hosta 'Opipara Bill Brincka'
Large, marginally variegated leaves.

Clump size & habit: 60 in wide × 28 in. high (150 × 70 cm). A rhizomatous, dense, unsymmetrical mound.

Description: Leaf blade 10 × 8½ in. (25 × 21 cm), of good substance, waxy, bright olive green, widely and fairly evenly margined rich yellow turning ivory, lightly dimpled, edge undulate to twisted, arching, oval with a recurved tip and flat to tapered, open lobes. Petiole shallow, short, olive green, outlined in cream. Flower rich purple-striped deep lavender on an upright, leafy, green, 30 in. (75 cm) scape in late summer; fertile.

Comments: Light to moderate shade. Rapid growth rate. Not suitable for containers. Flowers are held well above the leaf mound.

Similar: *H.* 'Opipara Koriyama'.

Hosta 'Ops'
Miniature, marginally variegated leaves.

Clump size & habit: 12 in. wide × 5 in. high (30 × 13 cm). A spreading mound.

Description: Leaf blade 2½ × 2 in. (6 × 5 cm), of average substance, satiny light green, irregularly margined deep cream turning white with some chartreuse streaking, widely veined, smooth, edge shallowly undulate, broadly oval

with a pointed tip and flat open lobes. Petiole open, shallow, green, outlined in near-white. Flower long, lavender, on an upright, leafy, green, 13 in. (33 cm) scape from early to midsummer; fertility unknown.

Comments: Good light to dappled shade. Best in a raised bed with other small hostas, ferns, and small heucheras, or as a container specimen. A vigorous, moderately fast-increasing miniature with a better constitution than many earlier introductions.

Similar: *H.* 'Dixie Chick'.

Hosta 'Osprey'
Medium, blue-gray leaves.

Clump size & habit: 36 in. wide × 17 in. high (90 × 43 cm). A compact mound.

Description: Leaf blade 7 × 5 in. (18 × 13 cm), of thick substance, light gray-blue with a hint of green, moderately seersuckered, widely veined, folded to cupped, widely oval to nearly round with heart-shaped overlapping lobes. Petiole pale gray-green. Flower bell-shaped, white, on a leafy, upright, pale gray-green, 24 in. (60 cm) scape in early to midsummer; fertile.

Comments: Takes two hours of morning sun in cooler climates, elsewhere prefers good light or light shade. Slow to increase. Pest resistant.

Hosta 'Pandora's Box'
Miniature, medio-variegated leaves.

Clump size & habit: 10 in. wide × 4 in. high (25 × 10 cm). A diffuse mound.

Description: Leaf blade 2½ × 1½ in. (6 × 4 cm), of thick substance, glaucous, palest chartreuse to creamy white, irregularly margined dark gray-green with paler streaking, dimpled, edge almost flat, cupped or convex, widely oval to nearly round with heart-shaped pinched to folded lobes. Petiole creamy chartreuse, distinctly outlined in green. Flower bell-shaped, pale lavender, on a leaning, bare, pink, 18 in. (45 cm) scape in midsummer; fertile.

Comments: Needs good light or high shade to retain the blueness of the leaf margins. Avoid direct sun. Establish in a container before

Hosta 'Pandora's Box'

planting out. Slow to increase; do not divide until the roots are fully developed. Reversion to blue-green leaves is all too common, so regular division is essential.

Similar: *H.* 'Cherish'; *H.* 'Cameo' and *H.* 'Hope' (leaves with the reverse variegation).

Hosta 'Paradigm'

Large, medio-variegated leaves.

Clump size & habit: 47 in. wide × 20 in. high (117 × 50 cm). A dense mound.

Description: Leaf blade 10¾ × 9 in. (27 × 23 cm), of thick substance, chartreuse-green turning yellow, widely margined dark green with chartreuse streaking, satiny above and glaucous below, intensely seersuckered and puckered, edge almost flat to slightly rippled, folded to cupped, widely oval with heart-shaped pinched to overlapping lobes. Petiole light green. Flower palest lavender to near-white on an upright, leafy, chartreuse, 20 in. (50 cm) scape in late summer; fertile.

Comments: Lutescent. Tolerates two hours of morning sun in cooler climates, but the color is more likely to fade. Rapid growth rate. Pest resistant. Divide frequently.

Similar: **H.* 'Dick Ward', **H.* 'Inniswood', **H.* 'September Sun'.

Hosta 'Paradise Joyce'

Medium, medio-variegated leaves.

Clump size & habit: 36 in. wide × 16 in. high (90 × 40 cm). A mound of overlapping leaves.

Description: Leaf blade 6½ × 4 in. (16 × 10 cm), of good substance, smooth, medium yellow then ivory, irregularly margined blue with paler streaking, matt above and glaucous below, edge almost flat, slightly cupped, oval with heart-shaped pinched lobes. Petiole chartreuse-yellow, outlined in blue. Flower bell-shaped, near-white, in a dense raceme on a thick, upright, bare, mauve-gray, 22 in. (55 cm) scape in midsummer; fertile.

Comments: Needs full sun in cooler climates for stronger leaf coloring, elsewhere shade.

Hosta 'Paradigm'

Hosta 'Paradise Joyce'

Moderate to fast growth rate. Easy to cultivate. A superb foreground specimen. Lovely in containers. Divide frequently.

Similar: *H.* 'June', *H.* 'Katherine Lewis'.

Hosta 'Patriot'

Medium to large, marginally variegated leaves.

Clump size & habit: 51 in. wide × 20 in. high (127 × 50 cm). A dense mound.

Description: Leaf blade 6½ × 5 in. (16 × 13 cm), of good substance, dark green, widely and irregularly margined ivory turning white with gray-green streaks, satiny above and glaucous below, dimpled, edge slightly rippled, widely oval with rounded, open to pinched lobes. Petiole dark green, outlined in white. Flower pale lavender on an upright, leafy, green, 28 in. (70 cm) scape in high to late summer; poor fertility.

Comments: Good light to moderate shade. Emerges late from rich violet shoots. Moderate to fast growth rate. A plentiful supply of moisture will produce wider margins. Superb in borders or containers. Named Hosta of the Year by the American Hosta Growers Association in 1997. Lovely with *Brunnera macrophylla* 'Jack Frost' and *B. macrophylla* 'Looking Glass'.

Similar: *H.* 'Minuteman'.

Sports: *H.* 'Fire and Ice', *H.* 'Loyalist', and *H.* 'Paul Revere' (leaves ivory to white with a dark green margin), *H.* 'Patriot's Fire' (leaves golden yellow with a narrow pure white margin).

Hosta 'Paul's Glory'

Medium to large, medio-variegated leaves.

Clump size & habit: 41½ in. wide × 24 in. high (104 × 60 cm). A dense mound.

Description: Leaf blade 9 × 7 in. (23 × 18 cm), of thick substance, chartreuse turning golden yellow, irregularly margined intense dark blue-green with some paler streaking, matt above and glaucous below, seersuckered, edge flat to slightly kinked, slightly folded or convex, widely

Hosta 'Patriot'

oval with heart-shaped pinched lobes. Petiole narrow, chartreuse, outlined in dark green. Flower pale lavender on an upright, bare, glaucous green, 40 in. (100 cm) scape in high summer; fertile.

Comments: Performs well in high temperatures, retaining its leaf color best in light shade. In summer the leaf center turns gold and the margins dark green; the center will bleach to ivory in hot sun. Medium to fast growth rate. Divide frequently. Named Hosta of the Year by the American Hosta Growers Association in 1999. Makes a colorful specimen or background hosta.

Similar: *H.* 'Inniswood', *H.* 'September Sun'.

Sports: *H.* 'American Glory Be' (leaf margin wider and blue-green), *H.* 'Chesterland Gold' (leaves entirely yellow gold), *H.* 'Orange Marmalade' (leaves with orange-gold central variegation turning white), *H.* 'Pete's Passion' (leaf margin wider), *H.* 'Saint Paul' (leaf margin wider and blue), *H.* 'Wheaton Blue'.

Hosta 'Peanut'

Miniature, medio-variegated leaves.

Clump size & habit: 18 in. wide × 6 in. high (45 × 15 cm). A widely spreading, flat to arching mound.

Description: Leaf blade 3½ × 2 in. (9 × 5 cm), of good substance, matt chartreuse to ivory turning pure white, irregularly margined and randomly streaked blue-green, seersuckered, edge undulate, slightly cupped, broadly oval with tapered, open to pinched lobes which eventually become heart-shaped. Petiole flattish, ivory, randomly outlined with blue-green streaks. Flower bell-shaped, purple-striped rich violet, opening from a deep violet bud with white markings on the petal reverse, on a stout, upright, pale green to ivory, 16 in. (40 cm) scape, with variegated leafy bracts, from high to late summer; seeds rare; fertility unknown.

Comments: Good light to light shade. Ideal for containers since the leaves eventually become

Hosta 'Paul's Glory'

attractively heart-shaped exhibiting dark green flecking towards the margin. Moderate growth rate. The flowers are among the most spectacular of any miniature and the thin leaf tips are echoed in the leafy scape bracts. A superb tiny hosta. Won Best Seedling Award at the American Hosta Society's 2002 First Look event. Divide frequently.

Similar: *H.* 'Biscuit Crumbs', *H.* 'Cherish', *H.* 'Teeny-weeny Bikini'.

Hosta 'Pearl Lake'

Medium, green leaves.

Clump size & habit: 36 in. wide × 15 in. high (90 × 38 cm). A dense, dome-shaped mound.

Description: Leaf blade 5 × 4½ in. (13 × 11 cm), of average substance, mid to dark green with a gray cast, matt to glaucous above and shiny below, slight dimpling, edge slightly undulate, folded, heart-shaped with heart-shaped pinched to overlapping lobes. Petiole narrow, green. Flower bell-shaped, purple-striped pale lavender, in a dense raceme on a narrow, upright, leafy, light green, 20 in. (50 cm) scape in early summer; fertile.

Comments: Dappled shade. Vigorous, fast-growing. Ideal ground cover or for woodland

Hosta 'Peanut'

Hosta 'Pearl Lake'

margins. Winner of the Alex J. Summers Distinguished Merit Hosta Award in 1982.

Similar: *H.* 'Candy Hearts', *H.* 'Drummer Boy', *H.* 'Happy Hearts', *H.* 'Pastures New', *H.* 'Saint Fiacre', *H.* 'Twiggy'.

Sports: *H.* 'Veronica Lake' (leaf margin creamy).

Hosta 'Percy'

Medium, marginally variegated leaves.

Clump size & habit: 36 in. wide × 15 in. high (90 ×38 cm). A dense, upright mound of cascading leaves.

Description: Leaf blade 7½ × 4 in. (19 × 10 cm), of average substance, medium to dark green, very widely and irregularly margined rich yellow turning ivory white with some chartreuse streaking, matt above and satiny below, veins closely ribbed, edge almost flat, slightly convex, oval graduating to a pointed tip, lobes heart-shaped and pinched. Petiole dark green, outlined

in yellow to ivory. Flower lavender on an upright, leafy, green, 20 in. (50 cm) scape in midsummer; fertility unknown.

Comments: Site in the midground of a shaded border or in light woodland, surrounded by plainer leaved plants to accentuate and frame its strikingly variegated foliage. Increases rapidly.

Hosta 'Pewter Frost'

Medium, blue-gray leaves.

Clump size & habit: 41 in. wide × 13 in. high (102 × 33 cm). An upright mound.

Description: Leaf blade 10 × 7 in. (25 × 18 cm), of moderate substance, intense blue-gray, prominently veined, edge slightly undulate, slightly arching, oval with a graceful tip and heart-shaped pinched lobes. Petiole glaucous light green, with random purple dotting. Flower long, near-white, on an upright or leaning, leafy, glaucous light green, 33 in. (83 cm) scape in high to late summer; fertile.

Hosta 'Percy'

Hosta 'Pewter Frost'

Hosta 'Pewterware'

Comments: Light shade. The thick glaucous bloom soon disappears, giving a gunmetal-like appearance. Moderate growth rate.

Hosta 'Pewterware'
Small, blue-gray leaves.

Clump size & habit: 24 in. wide × 8 in. high (60 × 20 cm). A dense, dome-shaped mound.

Description: Leaf blade 5½ × 4½ in. (14 × 11 cm), very thick, glaucous gray-blue, prominently and widely veined, edge widely undulate, heart-shaped to almost round with a vestigial tip and heart-shaped pinched lobes. Petiole long, deeply channeled, light gray-green. Flower bell-shaped, lavender-striped near-white, on an upright, glaucous light green, bare, 14–19 in. (35–48 cm) scape in early autumn; seedpods green; fertility unknown.

Comments: Dappled to full shade. The heavy glaucous bloom holds nearly all summer in hotter regions. Slow to increase. Pest resistant. Superb.

Hosta 'Phantom'
Medium, gray-green leaves.

Clump size & habit: 33 in. wide × 18 in. high (83 × 45 cm). A moderately dense mound.

Description: Leaf blade 10 × 7½ in. (25 × 19 cm), of good substance, waxy dark gray-green, glaucous light green below, widely veined, slightly dimpled, edge rippled, arching, oval with a prominent, extended tip and round to heart-shaped open to pinched lobes. Petiole green, with reds dots and a red backing. Flower densely packed, near bell-shaped, lavender, opening from a rich violet bud, on a leaning to upright, leafy, glaucous mauve-purple, 32¾ in. (82 cm) scape in late summer; sterile.

Comments: Good light to dappled shade. Of moderate increase. Not showy but nonetheless extremely gardenworthy. Site at eye level to best appreciate the ghostly gray-coated leaves and the intensely red-dotted and -backed petioles.

Similar: *H. pycnophylla*.

Hosta 'Phantom'

Hosta 'Piedmont Gold'

Large, yellowish leaves.

Clump size & habit: 36 in. wide × 24 in. high (90 × 60 cm). A mound of overlapping leaves.

Description: Leaf blade 8 × 6 in. (20 × 15 cm), of thick substance, chartreuse soon turning golden yellow, matt above and thinly glaucous below, prominently veined, dimpled when mature, edge slightly undulate, arching, convex, oblong to broadly oval with heart-shaped pinched lobes. Petiole deeply channeled, chartreuse. Flower near-white on an upright or leaning, bare, gray-chartreuse, 30 in. (75 cm) scape in midsummer; fertile.

Comments: Lutescent. Bright light but not direct sun enhances the leaf color; however, the color assumes a paler hue in autumn. Slow to moderate growth rate; becomes much larger given optimum growing conditions. Pest resistant. Leaves of juvenile plants are smooth.

Similar: *H.* 'Solar Flare'.

Sports: *H.* 'David Stone', *H.* 'Moonshine', and *H.* 'Summer Serenade' (leaves yellow with a green margin), *H.* 'Everglades' and *H.* 'Tyler's Treasure' (leaves green with a gold margin), *H.* 'Lakeside Symphony' (leaves yellow with a muted chartreuse margin), **H.* 'Satisfaction', *H.* 'Summer Serenade' (leaf margin dark olive green).

Hosta 'Pilgrim'

Small, marginally variegated leaves.

Clump size & habit: 20¾ in. wide × 8½ in. high (52 × 21 cm). A dense mound.

Description: Leaf blade 4 × 3 in. (10 × 8 cm), of average substance, matt, gray-green to dark green, very widely and irregularly margined yellow turning creamy white with paler green streaking, veins ribbed, edge flat to occasionally kinked, widely oval with flat to heart-shaped open to pinched lobes. Petiole green, very finely outlined in cream. Flower lavender on an upright, bare, dark green, 20¾ in. (52 cm) scape in midsummer; fertile.

Comments: Good light to moderate shade. Vigorous, fast growing. Easily exceeds its registered dimensions. Excellent as a specimen or at the front of a border. Good in containers.

Hosta 'Piedmont Gold'

Similar: *H.* 'Cherub', *H.* 'Moon River', *H.* 'Pixie Vamp'.

Sports: *H.* 'Pilgrim's Progress' (leaf margin up to 2 in. [5 cm] wide providing even more dramatic contrast).

Hosta 'Pineapple Poll'

Medium, gray-green leaves.

Clump size & habit: 45½ in. wide × 18 in. high (114 × 45 cm). An open, rippling mound of upward- and outward-pointing leaves.

Description: Leaf blade 9 × 3½ in. (23 × 9 cm), of thick substance, smooth, green with a gray cast, edge conspicuously rippled, slightly twisted, widely lanceolate with an acute tip and tapered, open lobes. Petiole flattish, light green. Flower purple-striped near-white on an upright, leafy, heavily glaucous green, 34¾ in. (87 cm) scape in late summer; fertile.

Comments: Light to full shade. A rapid grower. The leaf mound resembles the tuft at the top of a pineapple. Plant to contrast with strikingly variegated green-leaved hostas.

Similar: *H.* 'Blue Arrow', *H.* 'Hadspen Heron'.

Sports: *H.* 'Pineapple Upside Down Cake' (leaves chartreuse to rich golden yellow with a dark green margin).

Hosta 'Pineapple Poll'

Hosta 'Pilgrim'

Hosta plantaginea

Hosta plantaginea

Large, green leaves.

Clump size & habit: 60 in. wide × 24 in. high (150 × 60 cm). A dome-shaped mound.

Description: Leaf blade 11 × 7 in. (28 × 18 cm), of thin substance, pale to midgreen, satiny above and glossy below, veins widely ribbed, slightly dimpled when mature, edge slightly rippled, arching, oval with heart-shaped pinched lobes. Petiole midgreen. Flower very long-tubed, up to 5 in. (13 cm), exceedingly fragrant, white, on an upright to leaning, leafy, chartreuse, 32 in. (80 cm) scape from late summer to autumn; fertile.

Comments: Leaves turn chartreuse in sun. Tolerates morning sun in hot, humid areas and full sun all day elsewhere given enough water. Leaves unfurl slowly. Feed and water throughout the growing season. Has intensely fragrant, nocturnal, waxy, long-tubed white flowers. Zones 3–9.

Similar: *H. 'Royal Standard'.

Sports: *H. plantaginea* 'Aphrodite' (extra petals create the effect of a double flower, requires a hot, humid climate for the flowers to open, in cooler climates the buds usually abort before flowering), *H. plantaginea* 'Grandiflora' (leaves more lax, flowers with an even longer tube), *H. plantaginea* 'Ming Treasure' (leaf margin changes from chartreuse to white), *H. plantaginea* 'Venus' (flower a true double and more effective), *H. plantaginea* 'White Swan' (similar to the typical species).

Hosta 'Pole Cat'

Medium, medio-variegated leaves.

Clump size & habit: 36 in. wide × 17 in. high (90 × 43 cm). A dense mound.

Description: Leaf blade 7 × 5½ in. (18 × 14 cm), of average substance, pure white, very widely and irregularly margined mid to dark green, partially narrowly banded in chartreuse with chartreuse streaks, matt above and glaucous below, moderately seersuckered, edge almost flat, broadly oval with a pointed tip and heart-shaped pinched to folded lobes. Petiole ivory, outlined in dark green. Flower pinkish lavender, opening from a rich violet bud, in a dense raceme on an upright, leafy, gray-green, 23 in. (58 cm) scape, purple-tinted towards the raceme, in high summer; fertility unknown.

Comments: Good light to partial shade. Leaves emerge early. Vigorous. The early season blue cast to the green margin gradually disappears but can be enjoyed for longer if protected from sunlight. Correctly sited the white variegation holds the whole season. Divide frequently. Lovely with variegated *Actaea simplex*.

Similar: *H.* 'Risky Business'.

Hosta 'Popo'

Miniature, blue-gray leaves.

Clump size & habit: 15 in. wide × 7 in. high (38 × 18 cm). A dense mound.

Description: Leaf blade 2 × 1½ in. (5 × 4 cm), of good substance, light blue-gray turning green, smooth, edge flat, slightly folded, widely oval with tapered lobes. Petiole gray-green. Flower

pale lavender to near-white on an upright, bare, light green, 12 in. (30 cm) scape in late summer; fertile.

Comments: Needs morning sun in cooler climates to boost the vigor, then light shade. Ideal for rock gardens, sinks, and containers.

Hosta 'Pole Cat'

Hosta 'Popo'

Similar: *H.* 'Peedee Graymulkin' (leaves rounder, thicker, with a distinct vestigial tip).

Hosta 'Potomac Pride'
Large, green leaves.

Clump size & habit: 49 in. wide × 28 in. high (122 × 70 cm). A rounded, semi-upright mound.

Hosta 'Potomac Pride'

Description: Leaf blade 12 × 8 in. (30 × 20 cm), of thick substance, leathery, very dark green with a blue cast, glossy above and a powdery bloom below, crumpled and puckered, veins ribbed, edge almost flat to slightly rippled, mostly convex, widely oval with rounded, open to pinched lobes. Petiole pale green. Flower small, spider-shaped, lavender, on an upright, leafy, pale green, 34 in. (85 cm) scape in mid to late summer; fertile.

Comments: Performs equally well in hot or cooler regions. Full sun for a half to three-quarters of the day. Vigorous, fast growing. A superb hosta that improves with each succeeding summer.

Similar: *H.* 'Flower Power'.

Sports: *H.* 'Capitol Hill' (leaf margin greenish yellow).

Hosta 'Powder Blue'
Large, very blue leaves.

Clump size & habit: 60 in. wide × 27 in. high (150 × 68 cm). A rounded mound.

Description: Leaf blade 14 × 10¾ in. (35 × 27 cm), of thick substance, emerges chartreuse

Hosta 'Powder Blue'

becoming light powder blue, powdery above and heavily glaucous below, deeply and closely seersuckered, edge with slight undulations, lightly cupped, widely oval to heart-shaped with pinched to folded lobes. Petiole stout, light blue. Flower bell-shaped, pale lavender, on an upright, leafy, 34½ in. (86 cm) scape from early to mid-summer; fertile.

Comments: Tolerates hot, humid conditions and excessive rainfall but best in cooler gardens sited in moderate shade to maintain the almost unearthly leaf coloring and texture. The attractive flower trusses are noticeable for their length. Pest resistant. Grow with lacy ferns and other contrasting dark green foliage or as a specimen where the powdered leaves with their suedelike finish will be best appreciated.

Hosta 'Prairie Sky'

Small to medium, very blue leaves.

Clump size & habit: 36 in. wide × 14 in. high (90 × 35 cm). A compact mound.

Description: Leaf blade 7 × 6 in. (18 × 15 cm), of thick substance, glaucous powdery blue, dim-pled to seersuckered, edge flat, lightly cupped, broadly oval with a vestigial tip and heart-shaped pinched lobes. Petiole lighter blue. Flower near-white to pale lavender on an upright to leaning 18–24 in. (45–60 cm) scape from mid to late summer; fertility unknown.

Comments: Best in shade where lower light levels help retain the best leaf color, but not under trees where raindrops and falling debris might cause damage. Moderately vigorous.

Similar: *H.* 'Blue Danube' (leaves darker).

Hosta 'Prince of Wales'

Giant, gray-green leaves.

Clump size & habit: 71 in. wide × 36 in. high (178 × 90 cm). A stately, dense mound.

Description: Leaf blade 20¾ × 14 in. (52 × 35 cm), of thick substance, silvery gray-green with a slight blue cast in early season, seersuckered, strongly veined, edge slightly undulate, slightly arching, elliptic to oval with heart-shaped overlapping lobes. Petiole leaning, stout, grayish white. Flower lavender-gray in a heavy truss on an upright to leaning, swan-necked, leafy, glau-

Hosta 'Prairie Sky'

Hosta 'Prince of Wales'

cous gray-green, 35 in. (88 cm) scape in midsummer; fertile.

Comments: Some morning sun in cooler climates, light to moderate shade in hotter regions. Moderate growth rate. Purple-leaved *Heuchera* 'Purple Petticoats' provides an outstanding contrast.

Hosta 'Queen Josephine'

Medium, marginally variegated leaves.

Clump size & habit: 34 in. wide × 16³/4 in. high (85 × 42 cm). A vase-shaped mound.

Description: Leaf blade 7 × 5¹/2 in. (18 × 14 cm), of heavy substance, smooth, glossy dark green, widely and evenly margined golden yellow turning ivory, with some chartreuse streaking, veins conspicuous, edge almost flat, oval with a rounded tip and heart-shaped open to pinched lobes. Petiole dark green, outlined in yellow. Flower lavender on an upright, leafy, maroon-dotted, 16³/4 in. (42 cm) scape in late summer; fertility unknown.

Comments: Morning sun in cooler climates, good light or moderate shade in hotter regions. Increases rapidly. Pest resistant. A hosta with many attributes.

Similar: *H.* 'Abiqua Delight', *H.* 'Antoinette', *H.* 'Bold Edger', *H.* 'Cordelia', *H.* 'Don Stevens', **H.* 'Emily Dickinson', *H.* 'Goddess of Athena'.

Hosta 'Queen of the Seas'

Large, blue-gray leaves.

Clump size & habit: 49 in. wide × 24 in. high (122 × 60 cm). A layered mound of great architectural beauty.

Description: Leaf blade 11¹/2 × 9 in. (29 × 23 cm), of thick substance, intensely glaucous, rich blue-gray, veins furrowed, some seersuckering when mature, edge strongly rippled and slightly serrate, exaggeratedly twisted towards the tip, broadly oval with heart-shaped open to folded lobes. Petiole arching, glaucous blue-gray. Flower near-white on a glaucous blue-gray, slightly leaning, leafy, 27¹/2 in. (69 cm) scape in midsummer; fertile.

Hosta 'Queen Josephine'

Hosta 'Queen of the Seas'

Hosta 'Quilted Hearts'

Comments: Light and adequate moisture will accentuate the plant's characteristics. Winner of "Best in Show" at the 1997 American Hosta Society's National Convention.

Similar: *H.* 'Blue Piecrust' and *H.* 'Donahue Piecrust' (leaves less shapely and more poorly colored).

Hosta 'Quilted Hearts'

Large, gray-green leaves.

Clump size & habit: 46 in. wide × 20 in. high (115 × 50 cm). A dense mound.

Description: Leaf blade 11½ × 9 in. (29 × 23 cm), very thick, dark gray-green with a slight blue cast early in the season, matt above and thickly glaucous pale green below, seersuckered, edge almost flat, slightly convex, nearly round with a vestigial tip and heart-shaped overlapping lobes. Petiole stout, light green. Flower pink-tinted white on an upright, leafy, glaucous light green, 20 in. (50 cm) scape in late summer; fertile.

Comments: Light to moderate shade all day. Slow to establish but eventually impressive. Pest resistant. Intensely seersuckered leaves are shirred along the veins giving a pebbled effect.

Similar: **H.* 'Quilted Skies'.

Hosta 'Quilted Skies'

Large, blue-gray leaves.

Clump size & habit: 48 in. wide × 26 in. high (120 × 65 cm). A billowing mound.

Description: Leaf blade 13 × 10 in. (33 × 25 cm), of thick substance, intense silvery blue-gray, deeply seersuckered and puckered, edge slightly undulate, shallowly cupped or convex, widely oval to nearly round with deeply heart-shaped pinched lobes. Petiole stout, pale blue-green. Flower bell-shaped, palest lavender, on an upright, bare, pale gray-green, 30 in. (75 cm) scape in mid to high summer; fertile.

Comments: Good light to light shade all day. Slow to establish but eventually the heavy leaves droop downward and fold lengthways. Pest resistant.

Hosta rectifolia

Medium, green leaves.

Clump size & habit: 32 in. wide × 14 in. high (80 × 35 cm). An upright mound.

Description: Leaf blade 6½ × 2¾ in. (16 × 7 cm), of thin substance, midgreen, matt above and glossy below, veins ribbed, edge slightly undulate, convex, elliptic to oval, pinched at the tip and with tapered pinched lobes. Petiole green. Flower purple-striped bright mauve, opening from a darker bud, on a green scape up to 39½ in. (99 cm) in late summer; fertile.

Comments: Morning sun in all but the hottest regions. Scapes can tower to 7 ft. (210 cm) above the low foliage mound.

Similar: *H.* 'Decorata Normalis', *H.* 'Tall Boy' (flowers lavender).

Sports: *H. rectifolia* 'Chionea' (leaf crisply margined pure white with gray-green streaking), *H. rectifolia* 'Nakai' (leaves narrow with a creamy margin), *H. rectifolia* 'White Triumphator' (grown for its superb white flowers)

Hosta 'Red Hot Flash'

Small, medio-variegated leaves.

Clump size & habit: 21 in. wide × 14 in. high (53 × 35 cm). A dense mound.

Description: Leaf blade 12 × 2 in. (30 × 5 cm), matt gray-green to pale chartreuse turning greenish white, widely margined darkish green turning darker later with paler streaking, dimpled, edge slightly undulate, elliptic to narrowly oval with a pointed tip and tapered, open to pinched lobes. Petiole crimson-flushed toward the crown. Flower violet with white veins, on an upright, leafy, red-flecked midgreen, 22 in. (55 cm) scape from high to late summer; fertility unknown.

Comments: Suitable for hotter gardens in early morning sun followed by light shade. Grow

Hosta 'Quilted Skies'

Hosta rectifolia

Hosta 'Red Hot Flash'

with *Heucherella* 'Sun Spot' to echo the color. Moderate growth rate. The petiole is decurrent with the blade in juvenile plants. The margin varies from regular to irregular along its length and from leaf to leaf. Differs from its parent *H.* 'Peedee Gold Flash' in the thickness of the leaf, the much wider leaf margin, and the central variegation. The seasonal variegational changes provide attractive tonal contrasts. Zones 3–9.

Similar: *H. sieboldii 'First Mate', *H.* 'Lyme Regis' (flowers white).

Hosta 'Red October'

Small to medium, gray-green leaves.

Clump size & habit: 28 in. wide × 10 in. high (70 × 25 cm). An upright, open mound.

Description: Leaf blade 8½ × 3½ in. (21 × 9 cm), of thick substance, dark gray-green, smooth, veins closely ribbed, edge rippled to kinked, arching, widely lanceolate with an acute tip and tapered, open lobes. Petiole gray-green, with red streaks and speckles extending 1 in. (2.5 cm) into the leaf blade. Flower lavender in a dense raceme on an upright or slightly leaning, leafy, reddish, 24 in. (60 cm) scape in late autumn; fertility unknown.

Comments: Light to moderate shade. Among the best of the hostas with red petioles and scapes. Grow at eye level to appreciate the thick white coating of the leaf back. Companion plants include *H.* 'Tardiflora' and colchicums.

Hosta 'Red October'

Hosta 'Regal Splendor'

Large, marginally variegated leaves.

Clump size & habit: 36 in. wide × 34 in. high (90 × 85 cm). A vase-shaped mound.

Description: Leaf blade 11 × 6¾ in. (28 × 17 cm), of thick substance, glaucous gray-blue, irregularly margined yellow to creamy white with grayish streaks, veins closely ribbed, edge rippled, arching, oval with tapered, open to pinched lobes. Petiole light green, outlined in cream. Flower lavender on an upright, bare, light gray-green, 60 in. (150 cm) scape in mid to high summer; sterile.

Comments: Provide good light to light shade. Moderate to good growth rate. Pest resistant. A striking specimen. Very regal looking in antique stone containers. Named Hosta of the Year by the American Hosta Growers Association in 2003.

Similar: *H.* 'Jewel of the Nile' (leaves slightly smaller).

Hosta 'Resonance'

Medium, marginally variegated leaves.

Clump size & habit: 30 in. wide × 9 in. high (75 × 23 cm). A spreading mound.

Description: Leaf blade 6½ × 2½ in. (16 × 6 cm) of thin substance, dark green, irregularly margined yellow turning creamy white, matt above and shiny below, edge rippled, arching, widely lanceolate with an acute tip and tapered, open lobes. Petiole dark green, outlined in yellow. Flower lavender on an upright, light green, 20 in. (50 cm) scape in late summer; fertile.

Comments: Light to moderate shade. Rapid growth rate. Very susceptible to pest damage. Makes a useful ground cover. Not suitable for containers.

Similar: *H.* 'Austin Dickinson', *H. 'Candy Cane', *H.* 'Crested Surf', *H.* 'Gay Blade', *H.* 'Ground Master', *H.* 'Suzanne'.

Hosta 'Revolution'

Medium, medio-variegated leaves.

Clump size & habit: 41 in. wide × 20 in. high (102 × 50 cm). An upright mound.

Hosta 'Regal Splendor'

Hosta 'Resonance'

Hosta 'Revolution'

Description: Leaf blade 7½ × 4 in. (19 × 10 cm), of moderate substance, smooth, creamy ivory conspicuously flecked green, widely margined dark green with gray-green streaking, satiny above and glaucous below, edge widely undulate, variably oval or heart-shaped with a recurved tip and rounded, open to pinched lobes. Petiole ivory white, finely outlined in dark green. Flower pale lavender on an upright, leafy, green, 28 in. (70 cm) scape in high to late summer; poor fertility.

Comments: Some morning sun in cooler climates but not in warm climates. Requires careful siting to achieve the right balance of sun and shade. Differs from its parent *H.* 'Loyalist' in having green flecks in the leaf center. Divide frequently.

Similar: *H.* 'Pathfinder'.

Hosta 'Royal Standard'

Large, green leaves.

Clump size & habit: 51 wide × 26 in. high (127 × 63 cm). A dense mound.

Description: Leaf blade 9 × 5 in. (23 × 13 cm), of average substance, bright green, satiny above and shiny below, slightly dimpled when mature, edge slightly undulate, slightly arching, oval with tapered, open to pinched lobes. Petiole light green. Flower fragrant, white, opening from a lavender-tinted bud, on an upright to slightly leaning, leafy, pale green, 42 in. (105 cm) scape from late summer until autumn; fertile.

Comments: Morning sun in the hottest climates, three-quarters of a day's sun in cooler regions. Water and feed copiously through the growing season. Leaves turn chartreuse in full sun. Vigorous, fast growing. Very fragrant, waxy, white flowers are far more abundant on this selection than on its *H. plantaginea* parent. Flowers well in cooler regions. Zones 3–9.

Similar: *H.* 'Sweet Susan' (flower fragrant, slightly purple).

Sports: *H.* 'Hoosier Harmony' (leaves chartreuse to old gold with a dark green margin), *H.* 'Prairieland Memories' (leaves yellow), *H.* 'Royal Accolade' (central variegation does not persist).

Hosta 'Royal Standard'

Hosta 'Sagae'

Large to giant, marginally variegated leaves.

Clump size & habit: 71 in. wide × 30 in. high (178 × 75 cm). An impressive mound.

Description: Leaf blade 14 × 10 in. (35 × 25 cm), of thick substance, smooth blue-tinted midgreen turning gray-green, widely and irregularly margined bright yellow turning creamy white by midsummer with gray-green streaking, matt above and glaucous below, widely veined, edge widely undulate, flat to slightly folded, widely oval with a slender tip and heart-shaped open to pinched lobes. Petiole narrow, green, barely outlined in cream. Flower lavender, in profusion, on a thick, leaning, leafy, intensely glaucous gray-green, 49 in. (122 cm) scape in high to late summer; fertile.

Comments: Light to moderate shade. Emerges early. Slow to show its potential, but eventually forms a huge specimen. Named Hosta of the Year by the American Hosta Growers Association in 2000. Winner of the 1995

Hosta 'Sagae'

Alex J. Summers Distinguished Merit Hosta Award.

Similar: *H.* 'Silk Kimono', *H.* 'Victory'.

Sports: *H.* 'Ivory Coast' and **H.* 'Liberty' (leaf margin much wider), *H.* 'Clifford's Forest Fire' and **H.* 'Magic Fire' (leaf margin even wider with some streaking).

Hosta 'Salute'

Hosta 'Salute'

Medium, blue-green leaves.

Clump size & habit: 15 in. wide × 14 in. high (38 × 35 cm). A dense, semi-upright mound.

Description: Leaf blade 8½ × 4 in. (21 × 10 cm), of thick substance, smooth, intense blue-green, widely veined, edge widely undulate to kinked, twisted, widely lanceolate with an acute tip, tapered, open to pinched lobes. Petiole blue-green. Flower near-white on a drooping, leafy, glaucous green-blue, 24 in. (60 cm) scape from late summer to early autumn; fertile.

Comments: Light to full shade. Moderate growth rate. Pest resistant. The very pale, glaucous blue-gray undersides of the leaves are often visible because the leaves are held upright. Zones 3–9.

Similar: **H.* 'Blue Arrow', **H.* 'Pineapple Poll'.

Hosta 'Satisfaction'

Large, marginally variegated leaves.

Clump size & habit: 49 in. wide × 25–30 in. high (122 × 63–75 cm). An arching mound.

Description: Leaf blade 9 × 7 in. (23 × 18 cm), of good substance, satiny, very dark green, widely and irregularly margined rich gold with chartreuse streaking, closely veined, seersuckered, edge rippled, slightly undulate, arching, widely oval, heart-shaped pinched lobes. Petiole long, dark green, outlined in yellow. Flower near-white on an upright or leaning, bare, gray-chartreuse, 30 in. (75 cm) scape in midsummer; fertile.

Comments: The base color has a slightly blue tint early in the season if the plant is grown in good light to moderate shade. Moderate growth rate. The margin covers nearly one-third of the leaf blade, up to nearly 2 in. (5 cm), making this a strikingly beautiful hosta.

Similar: *H.* 'Tyler's Treasure'.

Hosta 'Sea Dream'

Medium to large, marginally variegated leaves.

Clump size & habit: 49 in. wide × 24 in. high (122 × 60 cm). A mound of overlapping leaves.

Description: Leaf blade 9 × 6½ in. (23 × 16 cm), of average substance, emerging green, soon turning yellow with a variable narrow white margin, matt above and shiny below, dimpled, edge shallowly undulate, arching, widely oval with heart-shaped open lobes. Petiole narrow, pale green, very finely outlined in cream. Flower pale lavender, opening from a darker bud, on an upright, chartreuse, 30 in. (75 cm) scape in late summer; fertility unknown.

Comments: Viridescent. Needs morning sun in cooler climates to give best leaf color, followed by good light to dappled shade in the afternoon. Thinnish leaves need protection from strong wind. Rapid growth rate. Flowers are held well above the leaf mound. Zones 3–9.

Similar: **H.* 'Electrum Stater', *H.* 'Golden Torch', *H.* 'Saint Elmo's Fire', *H.* 'Zodiac'.

Sports: *H.* 'Day Dream' and *H.* 'Winfield Gold' (leaves yellow).

Hosta 'Sea Lotus Leaf'

Large, blue-green leaves.

Clump size & habit: 60 in. wide × 25 in. high (150 × 63 cm). A stiff, oblique to upright mound of horizontal leaves.

Description: Leaf blade 9 × 9 in. (23 × 23 cm), very thick, blue-tinted green turning green, evenly seersuckered, edge flat, shallowly cupped, round with a vestigial tip and heart-shaped open to pinched lobes. Petiole stout, shallow, light green. Flower pale lavender on a leaning, leafy, light green, 24 in. (60 cm) scape in late summer; very fertile.

Comments: Dappled to full shade. Slow at first, vigorous when established. Pest resistant. The leaves have a distinctive shape.

Similar: *H.* 'Blue Umbrellas', *H.* 'Roundabout'.

Hosta 'September Sun'

Medium to large, medio-variegated leaves.

Clump size & habit: 50 in. wide × 24 in. high (125 × 60 cm). A dense mound.

Description: Leaf blade 9 × 7½ in. (23 × 19 cm), of thick substance, golden yellow widely margined midgreen with occasional streaks, matt above and glaucous below, seersuckered, conspicuously veined, edge slightly undulate, slightly cupped or convex, widely oval, heart-shaped pinched lobes. Petiole chartreuse, outlined in midgreen. Flower large, bell-shaped,

Hosta 'Satisfaction'

Hosta 'Sea Dream'

Hosta 'Sea Lotus Leaf'

Hosta 'September Sun'

Hosta 'Sergeant Pepper'

soft lavender to near-white, on an upright, leafy, glaucous grayish yellow, 32½ in. (81 cm) scape in high summer; fertile.

Comments: Tolerates considerable sun, which makes the coloring even brighter. Vigorous, fast growing. Easy to cultivate. Divide frequently. Pest resistant. Zones 3–9.

Similar: *H.* 'Lunar Magic', *H.* 'Lunar Orbit', **H.* 'Paradigm', *H.* 'September Surprise'.
Sports: *H.* 'Hub City' (leaves blue-green).

Hosta 'Sergeant Pepper'

Medium, marginally variegated leaves.

Clump size & habit: 36 in. wide × 16 in. high (90 × 40 cm). An open mound.

Description: Leaf blade 6½ × 5 in. (16 × 13 cm), of thick substance, matt, bright, pale green very widely and irregularly margined chartreuse turning golden yellow with some streaks, seersuckered, strongly veined, edge rippled, widely oval with a vestigial tip and heart-shaped pinched to overlapping lobes. Petiole olive green, widely outlined in creamy yellow. Flower lavender-tinted near-white on an upright, leafy, green, 22 in. (55 cm) scape in midsummer; fertility unknown.

Comments: Tolerates sun in all but the hottest climates. Because the leaf is more gold margin than green center, this hosta is best grown with plainer-leaved companions. Slow to moderate increase.

Hosta 'Shazaam'

Hosta 'Shazaam'

Medium, marginally variegated leaves.

Clump size & habit: 24 in. wide × 12 in. high (60 × 30 cm). A dense, unruly mound.

Description: Leaf blade 7½ × 5 ⅛ in. (19 × 13 cm), of good substance, dark olive green, very widely and irregularly margined ivory-chartreuse turning white with chartreuse streaks, matt above and thinly glaucous below, seersuckered, edge flat with occasional kinks towards the base, folded, wedge-shaped with a twisted and recurved tip, flat pinched lobes. Petiole dark olive green, finely outlined in ivory. Flower pale lavender on an upright, bare, green, 24 in. (60 cm) scape in midsummer; fertility unknown.

Comments: Morning sun followed by light shade. The ¾ in. (2 cm) margin is unusually wide on a smallish hosta. Vigorous and easy to grow. Best planted amid plainer-leaved plants to accentuate the contrast between the dark green center and the eye-catching variegated margin.

Similar: *H.* 'Honeysong', **H.* 'Wide Brim'.

Hosta 'Shiny Penny'

Hosta 'Shiny Penny'

Small, yellowish leaves.

Clump size & habit: 12 in. wide × 6 in. high (30 × 15 cm). A congested mound.

Description: Leaf blade 3 × 2 in. (8 × 5 cm), of thick substance, glossy, bright yellow turning copper-yellow later, smooth, ribbed veins, edge rippled, elliptic to oval, tapered, open lobes. Petiole short, nearly flat, yellow. Flower lavender on an upright chartreuse, leafy, 18 in. (45 cm) scape in late summer; seedpods chartreuse; fertile.

Comments: Needs morning sun to enhance the leaf color. Rapid growth rate. Pest resistant.

Similar: *H.* 'Peedee Absinth'.

Sports: **H.* 'Cracker Crumbs' (leaves yellow with a green margin).

Hosta sieboldiana 'American Halo'

Large to giant, marginally variegated leaves.

Clump size & habit: 71 in. wide × 22 in. high (178 × 55 cm). A dense mound.

Description: Leaf blade 14 × 10 in. (35 × 25 cm), of thick substance, glaucous, dark blue-green irregularly margined, yellow turning ivory white with chartreuse streaks, seersuckered, strongly veined, edge randomly wavy, widely oval with a recurved tip and heart-shaped overlapping lobes. Petiole stout, light green, outlined in ivory. Flower pure white on a bare, glaucous green, 22–24 in. (55–60 cm) scape in early to midsummer; fertile.

Comments: Tolerates morning sun in cooler climates. Slow to establish but eventually a huge mound. Pest resistant. Winner of the 2002 Alex J. Summers Distinguished Merit Hosta Award. Zones 2–8.

Similar: *H. sieboldiana* 'Barbara Ann', *H. sieboldiana* 'Northern Halo'.

Hosta sieboldiana 'American Halo', excess sunlight having removed the glaucous bloom

Hosta sieboldiana 'Borwick Beauty'

Large, medio-variegated leaves.

Clump size & habit: 50½ in. wide × 24 in. high (126 × 60 cm). An open mound.

Description: Leaf blade 12 × 11 in. (30 × 28 cm), thick, glaucous, chartreuse, gradually turning white through yellow, widely and irregularly margined dark blue-green with chartreuse streaks, conspicuously seersuckered, edge slightly undulate, cupped or convex, widely oval to nearly round with heart-shaped pinched to overlapping lobes. Petiole stout, ivory, outlined in blue-green. Flower pale-lavender-striped near-white in a dense raceme on an upright, bare, light blue-green, 27 in. (68 cm) scape in mid to high summer; very fertile.

Comments: The central variegation is lutescent or albescent. Best in cooler gardens. Exposure to sunlight, particularly in early summer, can cause the leaf center to scorch and melt out. Divide regularly.

Similar: *H. sieboldiana* 'Color Glory', *H. sieboldiana* 'DuPage Delight', *H. sieboldiana* 'George Smith', *H. sieboldiana* 'Golden Meadows', *H. sieboldiana* 'Jim Matthews', *H. sieboldiana* 'Kingwood Center', *H. sieboldiana* 'Queen of Islip', *H. sieboldiana* 'Super Nova'.

Hosta sieboldiana 'Dream Weaver'

Large, medio-variegated leaves.

Clump size & habit: 36 in. wide × 18 in. high (90 × 45 cm). A dense mound over time.

Description: Leaf blade 9 × 8½ in. (23 × 21 cm), of thick substance, chartreuse turning ivory white, very widely margined dark blue-green with chartreuse streaks, matt above and glaucous below, seersuckered, edge slightly rippled, slightly cupped or convex, widely oval to nearly round with heart-shaped overlapping lobes. Petiole ivory-green, outlined in dark green. Flower pale-lavender-striped near-white in a dense raceme on an upright, bare, light blue-green, 27 in. (68 cm) scape in mid to high summer; very fertile.

Comments: The variegation is more albescent than lutescent. Lower light levels will produce a

Hosta sieboldiana 'Borwick Beauty'

Hosta sieboldiana 'Dream Weaver'

more pleasing leaf color. Careful siting is needed. Makes an eye-catching specimen in the border. Slow to increase. Pest resistant. Divide frequently.

Similar: *H. sieboldiana* 'Great Expectations' (leaf margin narrower, not as dark blue-green, central variegation wider), *H. sieboldiana* 'Thunderbolt'.

Hosta sieboldiana 'Elegans'

Large, very blue leaves.

Clump size & habit: 51 in. wide × 26 in. high (127 × 65 cm). A dense mound.

Description: Leaf blade 14½ × 10 in. (36 × 25 cm), very thick, rich medium blue, intensely seersuckered and puckered when mature, edge almost flat to slightly undulate, cupped or convex, widely oval to heart-shaped with heart-shaped overlapping lobes. Petiole light green-blue. Flower pale-lavender-striped near-white in a dense raceme on an upright, bare, light blue-green, 27 in. (68 cm) scape in mid to high summer; very fertile.

Comments: Good light to light shade all day. Most effective, like all similar hostas, in cooler gardens where the color will be maintained for longer. Feed in early spring. Slow to establish. Pest resistant. Flowers are bunched at the top of short scapes that rise only just above the foliage.

Similar: *H.* 'Edina Heritage', *H.* 'Helen Doriot', *H.* 'Ryan's Big One', *H. sieboldiana* 'Gray Cole'.

Sports: *H. sieboldiana* 'George Smith' (leaves chartreuse to pale yellow with a dark blue-green margin), *H. sieboldiana* 'Great Expectations' (leaf margin greener), *H. sieboldiana* 'Jim Matthews' (leaves yellow with a dark blue-green margin and chartreuse streaks), *H. sieboldiana* 'Northern Halo' (leaves longer).

Hosta sieboldiana 'Eskimo Pie'

Large, medio-variegated leaves.

Clump size & habit: 36 in. wide × 24 in. high (90 × 60 cm). A dense, colorful dome-shaped mound.

Description: Leaf blade 9 × 8 in. (23 × 20 cm), of thick substance, yellow turning ivory to

Hosta sieboldiana 'Elegans'

white, irregularly margined glaucous blue-green with attractive tonal streaking in gray-green and chartreuse, seersuckered, edge almost flat, slightly folded or convex, widely oval with heart-shaped overlapping lobes. Petiole ivory, outlined in blue-green. Flower pale-lavender-striped near-white in a dense raceme on an upright, bare, light blue-green, 27 in. (68 cm) scape from mid to high summer; fertile.

Comments: Good light to high, filtered shade in cooler climates, elsewhere shade all day. Slow to establish but eventually vigorous. Divide frequently. Pest resistant. Seasonal changes in leaf color give this hosta a "painted" quality which responds to careful siting.

Similar: *H.* 'American Masterpiece', *H.* 'Beckoning', **H.* 'Dancing in the Rain', *H.* 'Jim Wilkins', *H. sieboldiana* 'Northern Mystery'.

Hosta sieboldiana 'Frances Williams'

Giant, marginally variegated leaves.

Clump size & habit: 51 in. wide × 32 in. high (127 × 80 cm). A dense mound.

Description: Leaf blade 12 × 11½ in. (30 × 29 cm), of thick substance, glaucous, blue-green widely and irregularly margined yellow turning creamy beige with some chartreuse streaking, seersuckered, strongly veined, edge almost flat,

Hosta sieboldiana 'Eskimo Pie'

Hosta sieboldiana 'Frances Williams'

Hosta sieboldiana 'Great Arrival'

slightly cupped, widely oval to nearly round, heart-shaped folded lobes. Petiole stout, light green, outlined in creamy yellow. Flower pale-lavender-striped near-white in a dense raceme on an upright, bare, light blue-green, 27 in. (68 cm) scape in mid to high summer; very fertile.

Comments: Margins remain chartreuse, the base color a darker blue if grown in low-light conditions. Provide light to moderate shade to prevent the edges from scorching. Edges can scorch even in full shade in warmer climates. Impressive in a large container but it will need dividing every three years. Slow to establish but very popular. Winner of the 1986 Alex J. Summers Distinguished Merit Hosta Award.

Similar: *H.* 'Alvatine Taylor', *H. sieboldiana* 'Aurora Borealis', *H.* 'Brave Amherst', *H. sieboldiana* 'Olive Bailey Langdon', *H. sieboldiana* 'Samurai', *H.* 'Wagon Wheels'.

Sports: *H. sieboldiana* 'DuPage Delight', *H. sieboldiana* 'Queen of Islip'.

Hosta sieboldiana 'Great Arrival'

Large, marginally variegated leaves.

Clump size & habit: 51 in. wide × 26 in. high (127 × 65 cm). A dense mound.

Description: Leaf blade 12 × 11 in. (30 × 28 cm), of thick substance, glaucous blue-green, widely and irregularly margined bright golden yellow turning cream-beige with chartreuse streaks, strongly veined, seersuckered, edge almost flat, slightly cupped, broadly oval to nearly round, heart-shaped folded lobes. Petiole stout, light green, outlined in creamy yellow. Flower pale-lavender-striped near-white in a dense raceme on an upright, bare, light blue-green, 27 in. (68 cm) scape in mid to high summer; very fertile.

Comments: Needs two hours of morning sun in cooler climates followed by light to moderate shade. Hot sunshine and very bright light turn the golden yellow leaf margin ivory and the glaucous blue center drab green. The subtlest tones of variegation can only be maintained in cooler climates with an abundance of moisture available. Worth time and trouble moving it around

until its potential is achieved. Slow to increase. Pest resistant. Not suitable for containers.

Similar: *H.* 'Alvatine Taylor', *H. sieboldiana* 'Aurora Borealis', *H. sieboldiana* 'Frances Williams', *H. sieboldiana* 'Northern Exposure', *H. sieboldiana* 'Olive Bailey Langdon', *H. sieboldiana* 'Samurai'.

Hosta sieboldiana 'Northern Exposure'

Giant, marginally variegated leaves.

Clump size & habit: 70 in. wide × 36 in. high (175 × 90 cm). A dense mound.

Description: Leaf blade 12¾ × 11 in. (32 × 28 cm), of thick substance, glaucous blue-green, widely and irregularly margined cream turning ivory white with gray-green streaks, seersuckered, edge almost flat, slightly concave or convex, widely oval with heart-shaped overlapping lobes. Petiole light green, outlined in cream. Flower pale-lavender-striped near-white in a dense raceme on an upright, bare, light blue-green, 27 in. (68 cm) scape in mid to high summer; very fertile.

Comments: Needs good light to high, filtered shade in cooler climates, shade all day in hotter climates. Slow to establish but worth the wait. Pest resistant.

Similar: *H. sieboldiana* 'Frances Williams', *H. sieboldiana* 'Northern Halo'.

Hosta sieboldiana 'Northern Exposure'

Hosta sieboldii 'First Mate'

Hosta sieboldii 'First Mate'

Small, medio-variegated leaves.

Clump size & habit: 32 in. wide × 14 in. high (80 × 35 cm). An arching, rippled, somewhat rhizomatous mound.

Description: Leaf blade 6–10 × 1½ in. (15–25 × 4 cm), of thick substance, chartreuse turning rich golden yellow, irregularly margined dark green, satiny above and shiny below, dimpled when mature, edge kinked to rippled, arching, lanceolate with an acute tip, tapered, open lobes. Petiole flat, chartreuse, outlined in dark green. Flower purple-striped lilac on a thin, upright, leafy, chartreuse, 25 in. (63 cm) scape from high to late summer; fertile. Zones 3–9.

Comments: Good light to light shade. A hot, humid climate will increase its already vigorous growth. Suitable for underplanting larger hostas or for edging. Differs from its parent *H. siebol-dii* 'Kabitan' in being more robust and easier to grow in most climates. Divide frequently.

Similar: *H.* 'Green Eyes', *H.* 'Moon Shadow', *H.* 'On the Marc', *H.* 'Peedee Gold Flash' (leaf substance noticeably thinner).

Hosta sieboldii 'Paxton's Original'

Small, marginally variegated leaves.

Clump size & habit: 30 in. wide × 12¾ in. high (75 × 32 cm). A dense, spreading mound.

Description: Leaf blade 6½ × 2½ in. (16 × 6 cm), of average substance, smooth, olive green, narrowly margined pure white with some gray-green streaking, widely veined, edge flat to just rippled, flat to arching, elliptic, acutely tipped, rounded pinched lobes. Petiole green, finely outlined in white. Flower widely purple-striped lilac on a thin, upright, leafy, 25 in. (63 cm) scape in high to late summer; fertile.

Hosta sieboldii 'Paxton's Original'

Comments: Morning sun or good light to light shade. Easy to grow. Eventually makes huge clumps.

Similar: *H.* 'Change of Tradition', *H.* 'Cotillion', *H.* 'Gaijin', *H.* 'Gloriosa', *H.* 'Silver Lance'.

Hosta 'Silver Bay'

Medium, very blue leaves.

Clump size & habit: 34½ wide × 13 in. high (86 × 33 cm). A dense, flat-topped mound.

Description: Leaf blade 7 × 6½ in. (18 × 16 cm), of thick substance, intense silver-blue; seersuckered, edge slightly undulate, folded to heart-shaped pinched to overlapping lobes. Petiole light blue-green. Flower bell-shaped, pale lavender, on an upright, bare, blue-green, 21–23 in. (53–58 cm) scape in high summer; fertile.

Comments: Good light to moderate shade. Moderate growth rate. Pest resistant. Lovely with

Hosta 'Silver Bay'

variegated dead nettle or yellow-leaved hostas. Among the best blue-leaved hostas.

Similar: *H.* 'Blue Fan Dancer'.

Hosta 'Silvery Slugproof'

Hosta 'Snowden'

Hosta 'So Sweet'

Hosta 'Silvery Slugproof'

Medium, blue-green leaves.

Clump size & habit: 41 in. wide × 16 in. high (102 × 40 cm). A dense mound.

Description: Leaf blade 7½ × 5 in. (19 × 13 cm), of thick substance, smooth, silvery blue-green, edge undulate, flat to slightly folded, widely oval with an acute tip, heart-shaped pinched lobes. Petiole gray-green, dottted with red. Flower bell-shaped, pale lavender, on an upright, leafy, gray-green, 22 in. (55 cm) scape in high summer; fertile.

Comments: Light to moderate shade. Tolerates some morning sun in cooler climates. Moderate growth rate. Very pest resistant. Scapes sometimes branched.

Hosta 'Snowden'

Large to giant, gray-green leaves.

Clump size & habit: 53 in. wide × 32 in. high (132 × 80 cm). An upright mound.

Description: Leaf blade 14 × 10 in. (35 × 25 cm), of thick substance, gray-green with a blue cast early in the season, dimpled, closely ribbed veins when mature, edge slightly undulate, flat to convex, oval, heart-shaped pinched lobes. Petiole gray-green. Flower white on an upright, bare, 48 in. (120 cm) scape in mid to late summer; occasionally sets seed.

Comments: Good light or moderate shade. Slow to establish but eventually magnificent. Good in containers if profusely fed and watered.

Similar: *H.* 'Krossa Regal', *H.* 'Prince of Wales'.

Hosta 'So Sweet'

Medium, marginally variegated leaves.

Clump size & habit: 22 in. wide × 15 in. high (55 × 38 cm). An open mound.

Description: Leaf blade 7 × 4½ in. (18 × 11 cm), of average substance, mid to dark green irregularly margined yellow turning creamy white, with chartreuse streaking towards the tip, satiny above and glossy below, edge slightly undulate to kinked, slightly arching, oval with a recurved tip, tapered pinched lobes. Petiole dark green, outlined in cream. Flower fragrant, pale lavender, on an upright, leafy, green, 22 in. (55 cm) scape in late summer to early autumn; barely fertile.

Comments: Morning sun then good light to light shade. Leaves much narrower when juvenile. Increases rapidly and soon reaches maturity. Superb in containers, sited near the house so that its fragrant flowers, which can last until the frosts in cooler climates, can be appreciated. Named Hosta of the Year by the American Hosta Growers Association in 1996. Zones 3–9.

Similar: *H.* 'Bold Edger'.

Hosta 'Stiletto'

Small, marginally variegated leaves.

Clump size & habit: 32 in. wide × 12 in. high (80 × 30 cm). A low, cascading, dense mound.

Description: Leaf blade 5½ × 1½ in. (14 × 4 cm), of thin substance, satiny, mid to dark olive green narrowly margined yellow to creamy white with chartreuse streaks, dimpled, prominently veined, edge distinctly rippled, slightly arching, lanceolate with an acute tip, decurrent with the ripple-edged, flattish, green petiole that is outlined in cream. Flower purple-striped on an upright, thin, leafy, green, 25 in. (63 cm) scape in mid to late summer; fertile.

Hosta 'Stiletto'

Comments: Good light to moderate shade all day. Rapid growth rate. Divide frequently to retain the rippled edges. Excellent for edging or ground cover. The intense rippling becomes less marked as the hosta matures.

Similar: *H.* 'Crested Surf', *H.* 'Wiggle Worms' (leaves narrower).

Hosta 'Striptease'

Medium, medio-variegated leaves.

Clump size & habit: 50½ in. wide × 20 in. high (126 × 50 cm). A dense mound.

Description: Leaf blade 8½ × 6½ in. (21 × 16 cm), of good substance, chartreuse turning yellow to ivory, widely margined dark green with a blue cast in early summer, with occasional transitional silver-white flecks, matt above and glaucous below, conspicuously veined, edge almost flat, slightly arching, heart-shaped to rounded, open to pinched lobes. Petiole chartreuse, outlined in dark green. Flower pinkish lavender, opening from a rich violet bud, in a dense raceme on an upright, leafy, glaucous green, 28 in. (70 cm) scape, purple-tinted toward the raceme, in high summer; poor fertility.

Comments: Careful siting needed to achieve the most pleasing leaf colors. Moderate to fast growth rate. Use as a border specimen or in a large container. Divide frequently. Named Hosta of the Year by the American Hosta Growers Association in 2005.

Sports: *H.* 'Gypsy Rose' (leaves smaller, more folded, with a brighter color contrast), **H.* 'Hanky Panky', **H.* 'Kiwi Full Monty', **H.* 'Pole Cat', *H.* 'Risky Business'.

Hosta 'Sum and Substance'

Giant, yellowish leaves.

Clump size & habit: 60 in. wide × 36 in. high (150 × 90 cm). A spreading mound.

Description: Leaf blade 18 × 15 in. (45 × 38 cm), of thick substance, light green turning chartreuse to muted gold depending on light levels, shiny to waxy above and thinly glaucous below,

Hosta 'Striptease'

barely dimpled, veins ribbed, edge slightly rippled, slightly cupped or convex, widely oval with a conspicuous tip and heart-shaped overlapping lobes. Petiole stout, shallow, pale green. Flower pale lavender on a pendent, chartreuse, leafy, 44 in. (110 cm) scape in late summer; fertile.

Comments: Lutescent. Colors best in sun, which it will tolerate for most of the day in cooler climates. Site in morning sun and give plenty of moisture in warmer climates. Can suffer from stem blight. Rapidly exceeds its registered dimensions and can become one of the largest hostas. Leaves emerge from mahogany-brown shoots. Winner of the 1990 Alex J. Summers Distinguished Merit Hosta Award. Named Hosta of the Year by the American Hosta Growers Association in 2004. Zones 3–9.

Sports: *H.* 'David A. Haskell', *H.* 'Eagle's Nest', **H.* 'Lady Isobel Barnett', *H.* 'Lodestar', and *H.* 'Titanic' (leaves green with a yellow margin); *H.* 'Domaine de Courson' (leaves satiny dark green with a blue cast); *H.* 'Green Gables' (leaves glossy, pale green); *H.* 'Parhelion' and *H.* 'Winter Snow' (leaves chartreuse-yellow with a white margin); *H.* 'Small Sum' (leaves medium-sized, waxy, bright yellow); *H.* 'Something Good' and *H.* 'Variable Sum' (leaves chartreuse-yellow with a green margin); *H.* 'Vim and Vigor' (leaves darker green).

Hosta 'Summer Music'

Medium, medio-variegated leaves.

Clump size & habit: 21 in. wide × 14 in. high (53 × 35 cm). An upright mound.

Description: Leaf blade 7 × 6½ in. (18 × 16 cm), of thin substance, matt, chartreuse turning pure white, widely and irregularly margined olive green with chartreuse streaks, dimpled to seersuckered, widely veined, edge very slightly rippled, twisted, convex, widely oval with a recurved tip and heart-shaped overlapping lobes. Petiole shallowly channeled, ivory, finely lined chartreuse with wider olive green edges. Flower pale lavender, densely packed on an upright,

Hosta 'Sum and Substance'

Hosta 'Summer Music'

Hosta 'Sun Power'

Hosta 'Sweet Innocence'

leafy, chartreuse, 30 in. (75 cm) scape in late summer; fertile.

Comments: Good light to light shade all day and adequate moisture. Moderate to fast growth rate. Protect from pest damage.

Sports: *H.* 'Dance with Me' (leaves yellow with a green margin), *H.* 'Lakeside Meter Maid' (leaves white with a wide, dark green margin), *H.* 'Last Dance' (leaves chartreuse-green with a pale yellow margin), *H.* 'Summer Breeze' (leaves midgreen with a wide yellow margin).

Hosta 'Sun Power'
Large, yellowish leaves.

Clump size & habit: 36 in. wide × 24 in. high (90 × 60 cm). A dense, upright mound.

Description: Leaf blade 12 × 6¾ in. (30 × 17 cm), of thick substance, chartreuse turning brassy golden yellow, matt above and thinly glaucous below, veins prominent, slightly dimpled, edge widely undulate, oval with a recurved or twisted tip and heart-shaped pinched lobes.

Petiole chartreuse. Flower lavender on a leaning, leafy, chartreuse, 36 in. (90 cm) scape from mid to late summer; sterile.

Comments: Although lutescent, it achieves its best color early, which holds until the frosts. Site in morning sun even in the hottest climates with high humidity, provided there is abundant moisture at the roots in high summer. Becomes much larger in optimum growing conditions. Pest resistant. In late summer the pale petiole appears to pierce the blade contrasting well with the brassy golden leaf color.

Sports: *H.* 'Abba Dabba Do' (leaf margin much wider), *H.* 'Paradise Power' (leaves golden yellow with a dark green margin).

Hosta 'Sweet Innocence'
Medium to large, marginally variegated leaves.

Clump size & habit: 24 in. wide × 12 in. high (60 × 30 cm). A colorful, undulating mound.

Description: Leaf blade 8 × 6 in. (20 × 15 cm), of thick substance, light green, very widely

Hosta 'Tambourine'

and irregularly margined ivory to white with gray-green streaking and splashing, slight dimpling, satiny above and slightly glaucous below, veins conspicuous, edge shallowly undulate, convex, broadly oval with a recurved pointed tip and heart-shaped pinched lobes. Petiole deeply channeled, dark green, outlined in ivory. Flower large, very fragrant, pale lavender, radially arranged on a thick, upright, pale green, 24 in. (60 cm) scape, with occasional large variegated bracts toward the raceme, in late summer; usually sterile.

Comments: Except in the hottest climates, full sun all day to produce the best leaf color and most prolific display of flowers; moisture at the roots is essential. Moderate growth rate. Superb in containers where its fragrance can be enjoyed, although this is less apparent in cooler climates. Differs from its parent *H.* 'Fragrant Bouquet' in having leaves of greater substance with much wider, better defined margins and greater pest resistance.

Similar: *H.* 'Crystal Moon' (flowers almost white).

Hosta 'Tambourine'

Medium, marginally variegated leaves.

Clump size & habit: 24 in. wide × 13 in. high (60 × 33 cm). A dense mound.

Description: Leaf blade 6½ × 5 in. (16 × 13 cm), of good substance, midgreen, widely and irregularly margined yellow turning ivory to pure white with chartreuse streaks, satiny above and thinly glaucous below, widely veined, dimpled, edge almost flat, widely oval with a thin tip and flat to heart-shaped pinched lobes. Petiole narrow, dark green, outlined in ivory, with a rosy mauve backing. Flower lavender, in a dense raceme on an upright, leafy, green, 20 in. (50 cm) scape in late summer; fertile.

Hosta 'Tardiflora'

Comments: Leaves assume a blue-green overtone in good light but not direct sun. Rapid growth rate. Makes a good ground cover.

Similar: *H.* 'Bold Edger', **H.* 'Emily Dickinson', *H.* 'Torchlight' (petioles burgundy red).

Hosta 'Tardiflora'

Small to medium, green leaves.

Clump size & habit: 26 in. wide × 12 in. high (65 × 30 cm). A dense mound.

Description: Leaf blade 6 × 3 in. (15 × 8 cm), of thick substance, leathery, smooth, dark olive green, satiny above and glossy below, edge shallowly rippled, oval with an acute tip and rounded, open lobes. Petiole narrow, olive green, with purple streaks. Flower lavender, in a dense raceme on an upright, purple-streaked, 24 in. (60 cm) scape in autumn; fertile.

Comments: Good light to dappled shade. Excellent for warmer climates as the leaves die down late. Pest resistant. Valued for its autumn flowers which are disposed around the scape. Use with low-growing asters, autumn crocus, colchicums, and *Saxifraga fortunei*.

Sports: *H.* 'National Velvet' (leaves somewhat heart-shaped with a velvety sheen), *H.* 'Tardiflora Honey Glaze' (leaves overlaid honey-gold).

Hosta 'Tijuana Brass'

Large, yellowish leaves.

Clump size & habit: 25–28 in. wide × 20 in. high (63–70 × 50 cm). A dense, unruly mound.

Description: Leaf blade 10 × 8 in. (25 × 20 cm), of thick substance, emerging chartreuse turning bright, brassy golden yellow with green undertones, shiny above and thinly glaucous below, intensely seersuckered and puckered, edge almost flat with occasional slight undulations, cupped or twisted, nearly round with heart-shaped overlapping lobes. Petiole olive

Hosta 'Tijuana Brass'

Hosta 'T Rex'

green. Flower pale lavender on an upright or slightly leaning, leafy, olive green, 32 in. (80 cm) scape in high summer; fertile.

Comments: Easily exceeds its registered dimensions. Makes a statement in any lightly shaded garden. Probably has the most puckered and unruly leaves of any yellow-leaved hosta.

Similar: H. 'Aztec Treasure'.

Hosta 'T Rex'

Giant, green leaves.

Clump size & habit: 80 in. wide × 30 in. high (200 × 75 cm). A huge, impressive foliage mound.

Description: Leaf blade 18 × 14 in. (45 × 35 cm), of heavy substance, matt midgreen with a slight blue cast, prominently veined, seersuckered and puckered, edge slightly undulate, oval with heart-shaped pinched lobes. Petiole thick, pale green. Flower near-white on a leaning, leafy, 34½ in. (86 cm) scape in early summer; fertile.

Comments: Light shade and plenty of moisture. Slow to start but eventually huge. Pest resistant. Lovely in a woodland garden among marginally variegated hostas. The immense, heavy leaves cascade downwards, becoming creased and pleated.

Similar: *H. 'Big John'.

Hosta 'Tutu'

Large, blue-green leaves.

Clump size & habit: 46 in. wide × 16 in. high (115 × 40 cm). An open, tiered mound.

Description: Leaf blade 9 × 7 in. (23 × 18 cm), of thick substance, dark blue-green, veins distinct and widely spaced, dimpled and puckered, edge evenly ruffled and intensely glaucous on the underside, slightly folded to cupped, oval with an elegant tip and overlapping lobes. Petiole narrow, light green, with purple dots. Flower lavender on a leaning, glaucous green, 43 in. (108 cm) scape in late summer; fertile.

Hosta 'Tutu'

Comments: Needs light shade to retain the blue-toned leaf color. Use as a specimen or in a woodland setting with *Asplenium scolopendrium*, its strap-shaped leaves affording a contrast but echoing the hosta's ruffled edges. Scapes are weighed down by the dense racemes.

Similar: **H.* 'Queen of the Seas'.

Hosta 'Ultramarine'

Hosta 'Ultramarine'

Medium, very blue leaves.

Clump size & habit: 40 in. wide × 18 in. high (100 × 45 cm). A dense mound.

Description: Leaf blade 9 × 6 in. (23 × 15 cm), of thick substance, rich powdery blue, intensely glaucous below, veins impressed, edge has a thin hyaline line, smooth, flat, oval with a pointed tip and open to pinched lobes. Petiole narrow, glaucous blue-gray. Flower pale lavender on a semi-erect, leafy, 24 in. (60 cm) scape in late summer; fertility unknown.

Comments: Moderate shade. Rapid growth rate. Reasonably pest resistant. The leaf veins resemble corduroy fabric. Both the raceme and scape have long white leafy bracts.

Similar: **H.* 'Elvis Lives', **H.* 'Winfield Blue'.

Hosta 'Undulata Albomarginata'

Medium to large, marginally variegated leaves.

Clump size & habit: 36 in. wide × 18 in. high (90 × 45 cm). A dense mound.

Hosta 'Undulata Albomarginata'

Description: Leaf blade 7 × 4½ in. (18 × 11 cm), of thin substance, midgreen irregularly margined ivory white with gray-green splashing, matt above and glossy below, slightly dimpled when mature, edge slightly rippled, elliptic with rounded pinched lobes. Petiole green, outlined in ivory. Flower narrowly pale lavender on an upright, leafy, ivory, 25 in. (63 cm) scape in high summer; virtually sterile.

Comments: Light to moderate shade. Vigorous. Susceptible to pest damage. Adaptable to many situations, especially for covering large areas. Often confused with *H.* 'Crispula', whose leaves are significantly more twisted and undulate.

Sports: *H.* 'Undulata Erromena' (leaves entirely green and slightly wider).

Hosta 'Unforgettable'

Medium to large, marginally variegated leaves.

Clump size & habit: 24 in. wide × 22 in. high (60 × 55 cm). An upright mound.

Description: Leaf blade 8½ × 7 in. (21 × 18 cm), of thick substance, dark green, widely margined and splashed chartreuse turning golden yellow, satiny above and glaucous below, dimpled, edge slightly rippled, folded or convex, widely oval with rounded pinched lobes. Petiole green, outlined in yellow. Flower lavender on a stout, upright, green, 31½

Comments: Good light to light shade. Moderate growth rate. Pest resistant. The contrast between the marginal variegation and the darker leaf blade is exceptionally striking. Superb.

Hosta 'Vanilla Cream'

Small, yellowish leaves.

Clump size & habit: 15 in. wide × 7 in. high (38 × 19 cm). A somewhat rhizomatous mound.

Description: Leaf blade 4½ × 4 in. (11 × 10 cm), of average substance, pale lemon-green becoming brighter yellow finally turning cream, matt above and thinly glaucous below, prominently veined, seersuckered, edge flat, convex or slightly cupped, nearly round with flat to heart-shaped open to pinched lobes. Petiole pale green. Flower lavender on an upright, bare, red-tinted, 12 in. (30 cm) scape in high summer; fertile.

Hosta 'Unforgettable'

Comments: Lutescent. Morning sun then dappled afternoon shade for best leaf color. Lovely with Japanese azaleas in early summer.

Similar: *H. 'Golden Teacup', H. 'Little Aurora'.

Sports: H. 'Heart and Soul' (leaves emerge pale green to chartreuse becoming creamy white with a dark green margin), H. 'Ice Cream' (leaves olive green with a golden yellow margin), H. 'La-dybug' (leaves bright chartreuse), H. 'Peppermint Cream' (leaves with a distinct midgreen margin), H. 'Pistachio Cream' (leaves dark green), H. 'Wylde Green Cream' (leaves yellow with a dark green margin).

Hosta ventricosa

Large, green leaves.

Clump size & habit: 51 in. wide × 22 in. high (127 × 55 cm). A symmetrical mound.

Description: Leaf blade 9 × 8½ in. (23 × 21 cm), of thin substance, smooth, dark spinach green, widely veined, becoming strongly ribbed when mature, shiny above and glossy below, edge evenly rippled to piecrusted, slightly convex with a distinct thin tip and heart-shaped overlapping lobes. Petiole deeply channeled, shiny light green, with purple dots, Flower bell-shaped, rich purple, on an upright then leaning, leafy, satiny, burgundy-dotted pale green, 32–38 in. (80–95 cm) scape in late summer and early autumn; fertile.

Comments: The only hosta to come true from seed. The very thin leaves can scorch at the edges in warmer climates, even if in full shade.

Hosta 'Vanilla Cream'

Hosta ventricosa

Flowers do not begin to open until the scape is fully extended. Zones 3–9.

Similar: *H.* 'Taffeta'.

Sports: *H. ventricosa* 'Aureomaculata' (leaves with a yellow center which gradually fades), *H. ventricosa* 'Aureomarginata' (leaves dark green, margined and streaked yellow turning cream).

Hosta venusta

Miniature, green leaves.

Clump size & habit: 10 in. wide × 2¾ in. high (25 × 7 cm). A dense, spreading mound.

Description: Leaf blade 1¼ × ½–¾ in. (3 × 1–2 cm), of average substance, smooth, mid to dark green, matt above and shiny below, edge slightly undulate, folded, widely oval with rounded to flat, open to pinched lobes. Petiole narrow, lighter green. Flower attractive, rich purple with a near-white throat, on a leaning, bare, ridged, 14 in. (35 cm) scape in late summer; fertile.

Comments: Light to moderate shade. Rapid growth rate. More suitable for containers and rock gardens than a border, where it is easily swamped by larger plants. Leaves vary in size and shape.

Similar: *H.* 'Paradise Puppet', *H.* 'Tiny Tears'.

Sports: *H. venusta* 'Awesome' (a typical but small form of the species), *H. venusta* 'Elsley Runner' (leaves more lance-shaped, clumping up very quickly, good in pots), *H. venusta* 'Kifukurin' (leaves green with a yellow margin), *H. venusta* 'Kinbotan' (leaves green with a thin gold margin), *H. venusta* 'Ogon Otome' (leaves yellow), *H. venusta* 'Suzuki Thumbnail' and *H. venusta* 'Thumb Nail' (like the species but with flowers in a different shade of lavender).

Hosta 'War Paint'

Medium to large, medio-variegated leaves.

Clump size & habit: 30 in. wide × 18 in. high (75 × 40 cm). An open, spreading mound.

Description: Leaf blade 11 × 8 in. (28 × 20 cm), of thick substance, chartreuse-yellow fading to drab green, very widely and irregularly margined

Hosta venusta

Hosta 'War Paint'

Hosta 'Wheaton Blue'

rich midgreen with abundant chartreuse streaks, some jetting towards the midrib, matt to glaucous above and shiny below, veins deeply furrowed, smooth, edge with small even ripples, arching slightly convex, broadly oval with a pointed tip and heart-shaped open to pinched lobes. Petiole stout, pale green, outlined in darker green. Flower pale violet on a leaning, leafy, 41 in. (102 cm) scape in early summer; fertility unknown.

Comments: Viridescent; the optimum variegation is achieved in cooler gardens. Light to full shade. Lovely in woodland with azaleas, rhododendrons, and *Milium effusum* 'Aureum'. Superb. Vigorous. Piecrust edges are not present

on young plants. The variegation gradually fades in a random manner. Divide frequently.

Similar: *H.* 'Fortunei Albopicta', *H. ventricosa* 'Aureomaculata'.

Hosta 'Wheaton Blue'

Medium to large, blue-green leaves.

Clump size & habit: 36 in. wide × 18–24 in. high (90 × 45–60 cm). A dense mound.

Description: Leaf blade 7½ × 5½ in. (19 × 14 cm), of thick substance, blue-green, seersuckered and puckered when mature, edge slightly undulate, convex, widely oval to near round with heart-shaped pinched lobes. Petiole leaning, light green. Flower pale lavender on an upright, bare, glaucous green, 40 in. (100 cm) scape in high summer; fertile.

Comments: Performs well in high temperatures, but leaf color is best when plants are grown in light to medium shade. Moderate growth rate. Pest resistant. Zones 3–7.

Similar: *H.* 'Perry's True Blue'.

Hosta 'Whirlwind'

Medium, medio-variegated leaves.

Clump size & habit: 41 in. wide × 18 in. high (102 × 45 cm). An upright mound of twisted leaves.

Description: Leaf blade 7 × 5½ in. (18 × 14 cm), of thick substance, pale chartreuse becoming ivory to bright yellow then fading to drab green, widely and irregularly margined dark olive green with chartreuse streaks, strongly veined, matt above and glaucous below, slightly dimpled, twisted, recurved at the exaggerated tip, kinked at flat open lobes. Petiole ivory-chartreuse, outlined in green, flat toward the blade. Flower pale lavender on an upright, leafy, glaucous gray-green, 20 in. (50 cm) scape, with occasional large variegated leafy bracts, in late summer; fertility unknown.

Comments: Leaf color varies with temperature and age of the plant. Some morning sun is beneficial. Vigorous and easy to grow. Makes a superb ground cover. Very distinct among centrally variegated hostas with its broad, twisted

Hosta 'Whirlwind'

leaves on long petioles and conspicuous green veining. Divide frequently.

Sports: *H.* 'Dust Devil' (leaves dark green with a chartreuse margin that turns creamy white), *H.* 'Eternal Flame' (leaves creamy white with green flecks and a wide dark green margin), *H.* 'Second Wind' (leaves dark green), *H.* 'Whirling Dervish' (leaves green with a very wide yellow margin), *H.* 'Whirlwind Tour' (habit smaller and without the markedly twisted leaves).

Hosta 'Wide Brim'

Medium, marginally variegated leaves.

Clump size & habit: 45½ in. wide × 18 in. high (114 × 45 cm). A dome-shaped mound.

Description: Leaf blade 8 × 6 in. (20 × 16 cm), of good substance, dark green with a blue cast, widely and irregularly margined pale yellow to cream with paler streaking, matt to glaucous above and thinly glaucous below, dimpled, flat to slightly folded, widely oval with a vestigial tip and heart-shaped pinched lobes. Petiole dark green, outlined in cream. Flower violet-striped pale lavender, opening from an attractive pale lavender-gray bud, in a dense raceme on an upright, bare, glaucous green, 24 in. (60 cm) scape in late summer; fertile.

Comments: Good light to high, filtered shade to retain the attractive leaf colors. Rapid growth rate. Very popular with flower arrangers because of the pleasing outline, the rugosity, the distinctive wide margin, and the contrasting dark base color. The leaf margin reaches up to 1½ in. (4 cm) in optimum growing conditions.

Similar: *H.* 'Honeysong', *H.* 'Mama Mia' (leaves larger).

Hosta 'Wide Brim'

Hosta 'Winfield Blue'

Sports: *H.* 'Cowrie' (leaves narrowly variegated with a very exaggerated brim), *H.* 'Stetson' (leaf edge wavy and conspicuously furled).

Hosta 'Winfield Blue'

Small, very blue leaves.

Clump size & habit: 45½ in. wide × 18 in. high (114 × 45 cm). An open mound.

Description: Leaf blade 7½ × 5 in. (19 × 13 cm), of thick substance, powdery blue, slightly dimpled, edge distinctly rippled, slightly arching, oval with an extended tip and tapered, open lobes. Petiole flattish, light blue. Flower palest lavender on an upright, bare, light blue-green, 28 in. (70 cm) scape in high summer; fertile.

Comments: One of the bluest-leaved hostas and quite distinct provided it is grown in light to full shade; the best results occur in cooler climates.

Similar: **H.* 'Elvis Lives'.

Hosta 'Wolverine'

Medium, marginally variegated leaves.

Clump size & habit: 38½ in. wide × 15 in. high (96 × 38 cm). A dense, cascading mound.

Hosta 'Wolverine'

Description: Leaf blade 10 × 5½ in. (25 × 14 cm), of good substance, smooth, blue-tinted green, widely and irregularly margined and splashed cream to white with gray-green streaks, satiny above and glaucous below, edge slightly rippled, arching, widely lanceolate with an acute tip and tapered, open lobes. Petiole flattish, green, faintly outlined in cream. Flower pale lavender on an upright, bare, green, 20 in. (50 cm) scape in late summer; fertility unknown.

Comments: Good light to moderate shade. Vigorous, fast growing. Use as a foreground specimen or in a tall terracotta chimney pot to accentuate the cascading leaves.

Sports: *H.* 'Curtain Call' (leaves rich, dark blue-green).

Hosta 'Woolly Mammoth'

Large to giant, marginally variegated leaves.

Clump size & habit: 60 in. wide × 27 in. high (150 × 68 cm). A dense, spreading mound.

Description: Leaf blade 12 × 9 in. (30 × 23 cm), of thick substance, glaucous light blue, very widely and irregularly margined chartreuse turning cream, intensely seersuckered, edge slightly undulate, broadly oval with heart-shaped pinched lobes. Petiole stout, light blue-green, outlined in creamy yellow. Flower near-white, opening from a lavender bud, on an upright, bare, 32 in. (80 cm) scape in mid-summer; fertile.

Comments: The margins do not burn, but the best leaf coloring is achieved in light shade. Rich,

Hosta 'Woolly Mammoth'

Hosta 'Xanadu'

Hosta 'Yakushima Mizu'

well-drained soil. Slow to increase but eventually huge. Pest resistant. The arching convex leaves accentuate the lighter midribs. Leaves fold and pleat towards the tip. Zones 3–7.

Hosta 'Xanadu'

Small, medio-variegated leaves.

Clump size & habit: 14 in. wide × up to 7 in. high (35 × 18 cm). A neat mound.

Description: Leaf blade 4 × 3 in. (10 × 8 cm), of good substance, matt ivory, widely and irregularly margined in three shades of green, darkest at the edges with lighter streaks, edge flat, lightly cupped, broadly oval with a pointed tip and tapered to heart-shaped open lobes. Petiole narrow, ivory, outlined in green, pink-dotted toward the crown. Flower purple-streaked rich lavender, opening from a pink bud, widely spaced on an upright, bare, 18 in. (46 cm), pink-tinted ivory-green scape; seedpods pink; fertile.

Comments: Some morning sun beneficial in all but the hottest regions, then light shade. Seldom suffers from leaf scorch. An attractive hosta for all climates if carefully sited. Differs from its parent *H.* 'Island Charm' in having greater vigor, much thicker leaves, and a significantly wider leaf margin with less streaking and splashing. Divide frequently.

Similar: *H.* 'Fantasy Island', *H.* 'Wylde Green Cream'.

Hosta 'Yakushima Mizu'

Miniature, green leaves.

Clump size & habit: 14 in. wide × 6½ in. high (35 × 16 cm). A flattish, open mound.

Description: Leaf blade 2¾ × ¾ in. (7 × 2 cm), thin, mid to shiny dark green, edge rippled, lanceolate with an acute tip and tapered, open lobes. Petiole pale green. Flower lavender on an upright, bare, green, 10¾ in. (26 cm) scape in late summer; fertile.

Comments: Light shade. Rapid growth rate. Flowers are sparsely disposed on the scape. Use in a rock garden or large trough.

Similar: *H.* 'Saishu Jima' (leaves slightly larger).

Hosta 'Yesterday's Memories'

Hosta yingeri

Hosta 'Yesterday's Memories'

Large, medio-variegated leaves.

Clump size & habit: 49 in. wide × 20 in. high (122 × 50 cm). A dense, flattish mound.

Description: Leaf blade 11 × 8 in. (28 × 20 cm), of good substance, chartreuse-green turning muted gold, widely and irregularly margined dark green with lighter green streaks, matt above and glaucous below, seersuckered, prominently veined, edge rippled, broadly oval with a short, pointed tip and rounded to heart-shaped open to pinched lobes. Petiole stout, chartreuse, outlined in dark green. Flower white-striped lavender, in profusion, on an arching, leafy, olive green, 35-½ in. (89 cm) scape in high summer; fertile.

Comments: Lutescent. The variegation remains a muted color even when exposed to sunlight. Ideal for hotter climates, even in sun, if plenty of moisture is available. Vigorous and easy to grow. Divide frequently.

Hosta yingeri

Small to medium, green leaves.

Clump size & habit: 30 in. wide × 9 in. high (75 × 23 cm). A compact mound.

Description: Leaf blade 6½ × 3 in. (16 × 8 cm), very thick, lustrous bright mid to dark green, glossy below with a white coating, smooth to slightly dimpled when mature, edge slightly undulate, arching when mature, oval to wedge-

Hosta 'Zounds'

shaped with an acute tip and rounded, open to pinched lobes. Petiole leaning, green, with purple dots. Flower narrow, spider-shaped, purple, on an upright, leafy, green, 25 in. (63 cm) scape from late summer to early autumn; fertile.

Comments: Good light to high, filtered shade except in cooler climates where it can tolerate morning sun. Moderate growth rate. Exceeds its registered dimensions in good growing conditions. Superb. Quite distinct for its glossy leaves and spiderlike flowers. Moisture at the roots is essential. Pest resistant. Zones 3–9.

Similar: *H.* 'Crystal Chimes' (flowers pure white and spiderlike), *H. laevigata* (leaves more undulate), *H.* 'Lakeside Looking Glass', *H.* 'Lily Pad', *H.* 'Sweet Tater Pie', *H. yingeri* 'Treasure Island' (a smaller selected form).

Hosta 'Zounds'

Large, yellowish leaves.

Clump size & habit: 30 in. wide × 20 in. high (75 × 50 cm). A dense mound.

Description: Leaf blade 8–10 × 8–9 in. (20–25 × 20–23 cm), of thick substance, chartreuse turning metallic golden yellow, satiny above and thinly glaucous pale yellow below, strongly seersuckered to puckered when mature, edge almost flat to shallowly rippled, shallowly cupped or convex, nearly round with heart-shaped pinched to overlapping lobes. Petiole stout, chartreuse. Flower pale lavender on an upright, chartreuse, leafy, 30 in. (75 cm) scape in mid to high summer; fertile.

Comments: Lutescent. Good light or moderate shade, where it will glow like a beacon among dark green-leaved plants. Usually exceeds the registered dimensions. Slow to moderate growth rate. Good pest resistance. Strongly veined underside of the leaf.

Similar: *H.* 'Abiqua Zodiac', *H.* 'City Lights', **H.* 'Tijuana Brass', *H.* 'White Vision'.

Sports: **H.* 'American Eagle', **H.* 'Dick Ward', and *H.* 'Laura and Darrell' (leaves dark green with a yellow margin).

USDA HARDINESS ZONE MAP

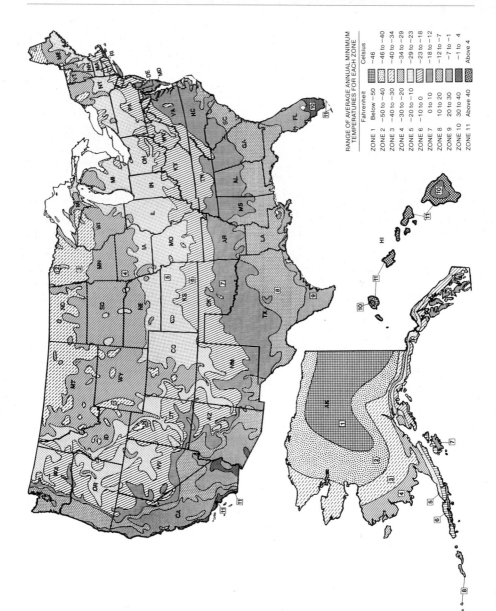

RANGE OF AVERAGE ANNUAL MINIMUM
TEMPERATURES FOR EACH ZONE

	Fahrenheit	Celsius
ZONE 1	Below −50	−46
ZONE 2	−50 to −40	−46 to −40
ZONE 3	−40 to −30	−40 to −34
ZONE 4	−30 to −20	−34 to −29
ZONE 5	−20 to −10	−29 to −23
ZONE 6	−10 to 0	−23 to −18
ZONE 7	0 to 10	−18 to −12
ZONE 8	10 to 20	−12 to −7
ZONE 9	20 to 30	−7 to −1
ZONE 10	30 to 40	−1 to 4
ZONE 11	Above 40	Above 4

EUROPEAN HARDINESS ZONE MAP

NURSERY SOURCES

Canada

Hosta Choice Gardens
4897 Irish Drive, R.R. #4
Appin, Ontario N0L 1A0
(519) 289-5471
www.hostachoicegardens.com

France

Le Jardin Anglais
Cantiran
47230 Montgaillard
33 (0)553 972 213
www.lejardinanglais.com

Netherlands

Marco Fransen Hostas
Paradijsweg 5
2461 TK Ter Aar
31 (0)172 602 031
www.hostaparadise.com

New Zealand

Taunton Gardens
Allandale
Lyttleton, RD 1
Christchurch 8012
64 (3) 329 9746
www.tauntongardens.co.nz

United Kingdom

Bali-Hai Mail Order Nursery
42 Largy Road, Carnlough
Ballymena, County Antrim
Northern Ireland BT44 0EZ
44 (0)28 2888 5289
www.mailorderplants4me.com

Bowden Hostas
Sticklepath, Okehampton
Devon EX20 2NL
44 (0)1837 840
www.bowdenhostas.com

Goldbrook Plants
Hoxne, Eye
Suffolk IP21 5AN
44 (0)1379 668 770

Mary Green
The Walled Garden
Hornby, Lancaster
Lancashire LA2 8LD
44 (0)1257 270 821
e-mail: Marygreenplants@aol.com

Mickfield Hostas
Mickfield, Stowmarket
Suffolk IP14 5LH
44 (0)1449 71156
www.mickfieldhostas.co.uk

Park Green Nurseries
Wetheringsett, Stowmarket
Suffolk IP14 5QH
44 (0)1728 860 139
www.parkgreen.co.uk

United States

The Azalea Patch
2010 Mountain Road
Joppa, Maryland 21085
(410) 679-0762
www.azaleapatch.com

Bentley Gardens
1817 Doverhill Drive
Lawrenceville, Georgia 30043
(678) 779-9709
www.bentleygardens.com

Cooks Nursery & Eagle Bay Hosta Gardens
10749 Bennett Road
Dunkirk, New York 14048
(716) 792-7581
e-mail: ranbl@netsync.net

Garden Crossings
4902 96th Avenue
Zeeland, Michigan 49464
(616) 875-6355
www.gardencrossings.com

Glenbrook Farm
142 Brooks Road
Fultonville, New York 12072
(518) 922-5091
www.glenbrookplants.com

Green Hill Farm
P.O. Box 16306
Chapel Hill, North Carolina 27516
(919) 309-0649
www.hostahosta.com

High Meadow Hostas
315 Township Road 15
Rayland, Ohio 43943
(740) 769-2447
www.highmeadowhostas.com

Hilltop Farm
3307 N. State Highway F
Ash Grove, Missouri 65604
(417) 672-2259
www.hilltop-gardens.com

Homestead Division of Sunnybrook Farm
9448 Mayfield Road
Chesterland, Ohio 44026
(440) 729-9838
www.hostahomestead.com

Honey Hill Hostas
3633 Honey Hill Drive, SE
Cedar Rapids, Iowa 52403
(319) 366-6613
www.hosta-holic.com

Hornbaker Gardens
22937 1140 N. Avenue
Princeton, Illinois 61356
(815) 659-3282
www.hornbakergardens.com

The Hosta Patch
23720 Hearthside
Deer Park, Illinois 60010
(847) 540-8051
www.hostapatch.com

Jim's Hostas
11676 Robin Hood Drive
Dubuque, Iowa 52001
(563) 588-9671
www.jimshostas.com

Klehm Song Sparrow Perennial Farm
13101 E. Rye Road
Avalon, Wisconsin 53505
(800) 553-3715
www.songsparrow.com

Kuk's Forest Nursery
10174 Barr Road
Brecksville, Ohio 44141
(440) 546-2675 (evenings)
www.gardensights.com/kuks

Lakeside Acres Hostas
8119 Roy Lane
Ooltewah, Tennessee 37363
(423) 238-4534
www.gardensights.com/lakeside

LandMark Gardens
17821 Pioneer Trail
Plattsmouth, Nebraska 68048
(402) 298-8884
www.LandMarkGardens.com

Naylor Creek Nursery
2610 W. Valley Road
Chimacum, Washington 98325
(360) 732-4983
www.naylorcreek.com

Northern Grown Perennials
54779 Helland Road
Ferryville, Wisconsin 54628
www.hostalink.com

Pine Forest Gardens
556 Ellison Road
Tyrone, Georgia 30290
(866) 605-5418
www.pineforestgardens.com

Plant Delights Nursery
9241 Sauls Road
Raleigh, North Carolina 27603
(919) 772-4794
www.plantdelights.com

Rice Creek Gardens
11506 Highway 65
Blaine, Minnesota 55434
(763) 754-8090
www.ricecreekgardens.com

Savory's Gardens
5300 Whiting Avenue
Edina, Minnesota 55439
(952) 941-8755
www.savorysgardens.com

Sebright Gardens
P.O. Box 9058
Brooks, Oregon 97305
(503) 463-9615
www.sebrightgardens.com

Shades of Green
P.O. Box 3134
La Crosse, Wisconsin 54602
(608) 786-0185
www.shadesofgreenusa.com

Vermont Flower Farm
256 Peacham Pond Road
Marshfield, Vermont 05658
(802) 426-3505
www.vermontflowerfarm.com

Wade Gardens
3867 Anderson Road
Bellville, Ohio 44813
(419) 886-2094
www.wadegardens.com

Walden-West Hosta
5744 Crooked Finger Road
Scotts Mills, Oregon 97375
(503) 873-6875
www.waldenwest.com

Walnut Grove Nursery
8348 E. State Road 45
Unionville, Indiana 47468
(812) 331-8529
www.walnutgrovenursery.net

White Oak Nursery
6145 Oak Point Court
Peoria, Illinois 61614
(309) 693-1354
www.whiteoaknursery.com

GLOSSARY

albescent becoming white.

bract a modified leaf usually at the base of a flower stem or sometimes forming part of the flower head itself.

crown the upper part of the rootstock from which shoots grow and to which they die back in the fall.

diffuse of a leaf mound that is wide-spreading but not dense.

dimpled of a leaf blade whose surface is pocked by small, round indentations.

drawstring effect the puckering of the edge of a leaf caused by the center of the leaf growing faster than the margin, which causes the margin to look as though it has been pulled tight by a drawstring.

fasciated a freak condition in which the stem of a plant becomes flattened, giving the impression that several stems have fused together. The flowers at the tip of such a shoot may also be abnormal.

floriferous free-flowering.

furrowed widely and deeply ribbed.

glaucous bluish green or bluish gray or covered with a bluish waxy coating.

hyaline line an almost imperceptible translucent to white line along the edge of a leaf.

hybrid the offspring resulting from the mating of two genetically different parents.

indumentum a thick, furry coating to the underside of a leaf.

jetting refers to variegation that sends streaks of color, beginning at the leaf margin, toward the center of the leaf.

lanceolate lance-shaped.

lutescent becoming yellow.

melting out where the center of the leaves of some hostas, especially those with white centers, first shows signs of scorching but then disappears, as though it has melted away.

mutation a spontaneous, vegetative variation from the original type caused by accidental changes in the genetic make-up of the plant. Such mutations are usually deleterious to the plant, but when they are decorative, they may be maintained in cultivation by vegetative propagation.

oblique of flower stems that lean away from the vertical.

pedicel the short stalk that connects a flower to a flower stem.

petiole the leaf stalk in hosta terminology.

puckering an exaggerated form of seersuckering, making folds in the leaf.

raceme an elongated, unbranched flower head in which each flower is borne on an individual stalk or pedicel, with the youngest flowers at the apex.

rhizomatous having underground stems that last more than one season and that often grow horizontally, producing new plants at the ends furthest from the parent.

rugose wrinkled, a term usually applied to the surface of leaves.

scape a flower stem that arises directly from ground level and bears no leaves. Used to refer to the flower stems of hostas which, though they may bear bracts, are without leaves.

seersuckered resembling seersuckered cloth, a lightweight cotton or linen fabric, and characterized by intense, even dimpling.

serrate toothlike indentations along the edge of a leaf.

sport a mutation.

subtended carried below: used of bracts on flower stems that are carried below the flower.

tetraploid having double the number of chromosomes of the typical plant.

transitional a line of variegation at the junction of the margin and leaf center.

undulate wavy, referring either to the whole leaf blade or to the margin. A margin can also be described as rippled or more closely piecrusted.

vernal spring.

viridescent becoming green.

FURTHER READING

Aden, P., ed. 1990. *The Hosta Book*. 2nd ed. Portland, Oregon: Timber Press.

Grenfell, D. 2002. *Hostas. RHS Wisley Handbook*. London: Cassell Illustrated.

Grenfell, D., and M. Shadrack 2004. *The Color Encyclopedia of Hostas*. Portland, Oregon; Timber Press; London.

Grenfell, D. ed. 2005. *Hostas*. Pershore, Worcestershire, United Kingdom: The Hardy Plant Society.

Schmid, W. G. 1992. *The Genus Hosta*. Portland, Oregon: Timber Press.

Wade, V. 2005. *The American Hosta Guide*. Bellville, Ohio: Wade and Gatton Nurseries.

Zilis, M. R. 2001. *The Hosta Handbook*. Rochelle, Illinois: Q & Z Nursery.

INDEX

Boldface indicates plants described in this volume.